Real Estate Investing

Steven M. Bragg

AccountingTools®

ISBN 978-1-64221-304-1

For more information about AccountingTools® products, visit our Web site at www.accountingtools.com.

Table of Contents

About the Author

Steven Bragg, CPA, has been the chief financial officer or controller of four companies, as well as a consulting manager at Ernst & Young. He received a master's degree in finance from Bentley College, an MBA from Babson College, and a Bachelor's degree in Economics from the University of Maine. He has been a two-time president of the Colorado Mountain Club, and is an avid alpine skier, mountain biker, and certified master diver. Mr. Bragg resides in Centennial, Colorado. He has written more than 300 books and courses, including *New Controller Guidebook*, *GAAP Guidebook*, and *Payroll Management*.

Steven maintains the accountingtools.com web site, which contains continuing professional education courses, the Accounting Best Practices podcast, and thousands of articles on accounting subjects.

Chapter 1
Introduction to Real Estate Investing

Introduction

A discerning investor can earn substantial returns from real estate. However, significant judgment is required to ensure that a property is of a sufficient quality level, that the price paid for it is reasonable, and that it is operated in a profitable manner. In this book, we cover the many techniques for finding and evaluating viable real estate investments, as well as how to finance, acquire, and operate these investments. In this chapter, we cover the types of real estate investments, how to acquire them, and which advisors to rely upon during the acquisition process, along with several related topics.

Advantages of Investing in Real Estate

There are several good reasons why it makes sense to invest in real estate. Consider the following items:

- *Below-market purchases*. It is sometimes possible to acquire real estate at a below-market price – especially when the seller needs to sell quickly, and you have sufficient cash on hand to fill this need. Taking advantage of these anomalies requires a deep knowledge of local market prices, which is easier to obtain when you commit to real estate investing on a full-time basis.
- *Cash inflows*. When a property is currently being rented out, it generates a stream of monthly rent payments. Some properties may have additional payments associated with them, such as for washers and dryers, storage, and parking. Depending on the offsetting cash outflows for mortgage payments, property taxes, maintenance, and so forth, the net cash inflows may be substantial.
- *Depreciation tax shield*. The depreciation[1] expense that can be claimed on a real estate investment involves no cash outflow, and yet reduces the amount of taxable income – thereby shielding you from a portion of the taxes that would otherwise be due. Currently, the depreciation period for residential real estate is 27½ years, while the depreciation period for commercial buildings is 39 years.
- *Property appreciation*. Depending on the area, real estate tends to appreciate – depending on local demand levels. This can vary substantially within even a short distance, but if you choose property carefully, it can appreciate quite substantially over a long period of time. Also, if you are good at fixing up real estate, doing so may trigger a substantial increase in property value.
- *Leverage effects*. Real estate is usually purchased with the assistance of a substantial mortgage, typically in the range of 70-80% of the purchase price. This

---

[1] Depreciation is the planned, gradual reduction in the recorded value of an asset over its useful life by charging it to expense. Land cannot be depreciated.

means that any returns from the property are magnified by the amount of this debt. For example, if you use a $50,000 down payment to acquire a $300,000 rental property and then earn $25,000 per year from it, you have generated a return of 50% on your $50,000 down payment – because so much debt was used to fund the purchase.

- *Tax deferral.* You do not pay income tax on any increases in the value of property until you sell it, which may not take place until years after the initial investment. In addition, it is possible under the current tax laws to roll the gain over into another real estate investment, thereby extending the tax deferral period even further. We discuss this issue further in the Like-Kind Exchanges section later in this chapter.
- *Rate of increase in income.* If it is possible to increase rental rates at the rate of inflation, then your income gradually increases, since the fixed-rate mortgage being paid off (your primary expense) does *not* increase at the rate of inflation. The following example illustrates the concept.

EXAMPLE

Sarah Henderson buys a single-family home for $300,000 that she plans to rent out. She makes a 20% down payment on the property and takes out a 30-year fixed rate mortgage at 5% for the $240,000 remaining amount of the purchase price. The ongoing monthly cash inflows and outflows associated with the property are as follows:

Mortgage payment	$1,400
Property tax	350
Maintenance, insurance, other costs	550
Monthly rent payment	2,600

Currently, Sarah is receiving $2,600 of rental income and paying out $2,300 for various expenses and debt repayments, for a monthly profit of $300.

In the following table, we note the results for Sarah over the subsequent 10 years, assuming that the rent payment and all expenses except the fixed mortgage payment increase at a rate of 2% per year, while the value of the home appreciates at a rate of 3% per year.

Year	Monthly Cash In	Monthly Cash Out	Net Cash Flow	Annual ROI*	Property Value
1	$2,600	$2,300	$300	6.0%	$300,000
2	2,652	2,318	334	6.7%	309,000
3	2,705	2,336	369	7.4%	318,270
4	2,759	2,355	404	8.1%	327,818
5	2,814	2,374	440	8.8%	337,652
6	2,871	2,393	478	9.6%	347,782
7	2,928	2,413	515	10.3%	358,216
8	2,987	2,434	553	11.1%	368,962
9	3,046	2,454	592	11.8%	380,031
10	3,107	2,476	631	12.6%	391,432

ROI = return on investment

The key takeaways from the preceding table are that the net cash flow from the property will gradually increase over time, and that the property value should increase substantially over time. Both of these factors should generate significant wealth for Sarah over the long-term. In particular, the net cash flows from the property increase so much that her return on investment doubles by the end of the 10-year period.

Disadvantages of Investing in Real Estate

Despite the positives noted in the preceding section, there are a few disadvantages to be aware of before investing in real estate – some of them significant enough to keep you from proceeding. They are as follows:

- *Grind it out.* The returns from real estate investing generally only accrue over an extended period of time, and only if you purchase judiciously and invest enough to properly maintain properties. Also, depending on the types of properties acquired and the nature of your tenants, it may be necessary to spend a substantial amount of time managing the properties.
- *Variability of income.* You may lose money in some periods. This is especially likely when only a small down payment was made, resulting in larger mortgage payments. Also, in periods when demand is soft, a property may not be rented at all or it will not be possible to raise the rental rate as much as you would like.
- *Unexpected maintenance.* There may be times when unexpected maintenance issues arise, such as a failed water heater or a leaky roof. The associated repair or replacement costs may be substantial, and could wipe out your cash reserves.

3

- *Rent control.* If you are investing in residential units, there is a possibility that the local government will impose rent controls, which severely limit your ability to raise rents.
- *Time requirement.* Investing in real estate requires a significant amount of time. You will need to spend time learning about the neighborhoods in which you want to invest, identifying problems with prospective investment opportunities, and dealing with maintenance issues. It is possible to hire a property manager to deal with tenants, but dealing with the property manager will still require a certain amount of time.
- *Transaction costs.* The transaction costs associated with buying and selling properties can be quite steep. These costs, which include commissions, title insurance, loan origination fees, and a variety of closing costs, can easily wipe out the appreciation in market value of a property. These costs can only be offset by holding onto properties for an extended period of time, so that they can appreciate to a substantial degree. A large part of these costs is the real estate agent's commission, which varies by type of property. The following table contains the ranges of commissions that are typically paid out for various types of property sales, with these amounts being split between the agents representing the buyer and seller.

Real Estate Commissions by Property Type

Property Type	Commission Range
Larger investment properties	1-3%
Raw land	10%
Single-family homes and condominiums	5-6%
Smaller multi-family and commercial properties	3-5%

- *Tax payouts.* Ongoing income from real estate, as well as gains from the sale of a property, are all subject to federal and state income taxes – which can be substantial.
- *Valuation declines.* It is entirely possible that the market value of real estate will decline sharply over the short term, especially when it was preceded by a bubble in property values that sent prices surging higher than the long-run trend. If you buy property near its peak price with a modest down payment, experience a valuation decline and then sell at the bottom of the market, it is quite possible that the entire amount of your down payment will be lost.
- *Rent declines.* During economic contractions, it can be difficult to find quality tenants. If the contraction is prolonged, you may be faced with ongoing mortgage, maintenance, and utility payments without any offsetting rental payments.
- *Leverage effects.* The leverage effect already noted as an advantage of investing in real estate can also be a disadvantage, magnifying your losses. To return to the earlier example of using a $50,000 down payment to acquire a $300,000

rental property, what if the result is a $25,000 loss in the first year? You will have generated a return of -50% on your $50,000 down payment, wiping out half of the investment. Thus, using debt to buy properties can very much work in your favor – or against it.

- *Liquidity.* It can be difficult to sell off real estate within a short period of time. This can be a problem if you have an immediate need for a significant amount of cash. When you are really pressed for cash, a vulture investor may swoop in and offer cash immediately at a steep discount to the market price of the property.

These disadvantages can be mitigated by holding real estate for many years, maintaining a cash reserve to keep you solvent during any negative cash flow situations, and rolling your gains from property sales over into new property investments (in order to avoid taxes). In short, there are disadvantages to real estate investing, but there are ways to keep them from overwhelming you.

Types of Real Estate Investments

There are several types of investment opportunities available, each with its own acquisition, operating, and tax characteristics that make it more or less attractive to the investor. Their characteristics are noted in the following sub-sections.

Purchase a Residence

The most basic real estate investment is acquiring your own residence. This can be considered an investment, because you will gradually build equity in the property as the mortgage is paid off over time. In addition, people frequently downsize once they retire, buying their retirement property for substantially less than the amount they received from sale of their prior residence; the difference can be used as retirement funding. In addition, a gain of up to $250,000 (or $500,000 for married couples filing jointly) is not subject to tax. To qualify for this exclusion, the taxpayer must have owned and used the home as a principal residence for at least two of the past five years. An option to take advantage of a reduced exclusion can be obtained by applying to the IRS. The IRS will consider situations in which a taxpayer had to change residences in less than the mandated holding period due to a job change or health reasons. If approved, the reduced exclusion is calculated as the ratio of the period of use during the past five years to two years.

EXAMPLE

A taxpayer is forced to sell his home after one year due to health reasons and move into an assisted living facility. The IRS approves his request for a reduced exclusion. The calculation of the reduced exclusion amount is 50%, which is one year of residence divided by the minimum two-year requirement.

Convert a Residence to a Rental

When moving to a new home, it can make sense to retain ownership of the old property and rent it out. This approach is most viable when you are staying within the local area, and so can more easily oversee the rental property. Another benefit is avoiding the transaction costs associated with selling the property. And yet another advantage is that you already lived in the home, and so are already aware of any maintenance issues it may have. In addition, the unit is now classified as an investment property, so that you can take a depreciation deduction, as well as deductions for all business expenses associated with it. These expenses include the costs to advertise the property rental, insurance, and maintenance costs.

A variation on the concept is to rent out a portion of your home. When this is done, the rent received is treated as taxable income. When you rent property for less than 15 days during the year and use it as a personal residence the rest of the time, you do not have to include the rent in your income; when this is done, you cannot deduct any rental expenses.

Upgrade and Sell Your Home

If you like fixing up homes, an investment option is to buy a home with maintenance issues, put time and money into upgrading it, sell the home, and move on to the next fixer-upper. This approach requires you to focus on upgrades that will increase the value of the home. Also, you must live in the home for at least two years in order to take advantage of the capital gains exemption of up to $250,000 (or $500,000 for married couples filing jointly).

EXAMPLE

Henry buys a fixer-upper home for $240,000 and moves in. Over the next two years, he spends $30,000 on materials, as well as many hours of his personal time, to make a variety of upgrades. Two years later, he sells the home for $360,000. This is a profit of $90,000 over his $270,000 investment, and represents a two-year return of 33%.

This approach is only recommended for those investors who like to deal with ongoing construction activities, find that moving frequently is not a burden, and are good at locating under-valued fixer-uppers. A final concern is that the transaction costs associated with continually buying and selling properties every few years can be substantial, and will offset a large portion of the profits generated.

Buy a Second Home

You may elect to purchase a second home and use it as a vacation home. You could keep the home only for your personal use. If so, the only investment return will be from the eventual sale of the property, based on any appreciation in its value. Offsetting this appreciation return will be the ongoing costs of purchasing and maintaining the home, including mortgage payments, insurance, property taxes, utilities, maintenance, and so forth. In addition, it may be necessary to hire a property management firm to watch the property. Generally, these ongoing expenditures more than offset any gains from property value appreciation, making a vacation home the least profitable of all real estate investments.

As was the case with your primary residence, you may elect to rent out the vacation home. When this is the case, the rent received is treated as taxable income. When you rent property for less than 15 days during the year and use it as a personal residence the rest of the time, you do not have to include the rent in your income; when this is done, you cannot deduct any rental expenses.

A variation is to rent out the vacation home the majority of the time, in which case the tax situation matches that of any other real estate investment. In this case, you are permitted to personally use the property for up to 14 days per year, or less than 10% of the days when the property is rented, and still take advantage of all the tax benefits associated with a rental unit.

The definition of personal use includes not only the days you personally use the property, but also your family members, the days you have donated for use of the property, and any days it was rented out for less than its fair market value. Thus, a donation of a week of time to a local charity auction would be considered personal use. Conversely, any time spent at the home doing maintenance does not count as personal time. Thus, if you spend a month fixing up a vacation home, it does not count as personal time.

Buy a Timeshare

A timeshare is a form of fractional ownership, where buyers purchase the right to occupy a unit of real estate over specified periods. For example, purchasing one week of a timeshare means the buyer owns 1/52nd of the unit. Buying one month equates to one-twelfth ownership. This model can be applied to many types of properties, such as vacation resorts, condominiums, and apartments.

There are many problems with timeshares that make them a poor real estate investment. In the following bullet points, we show why there are much better investments than timeshares:

- *Purchase price*. Timeshares are extremely expensive. Because you are only purchasing a fraction of the total time period for a unit, the developer can easily mask the fact that the price being paid is much higher than the market value of the underlying real estate.
- *Maintenance fees*. The maintenance fees charged for a timeshare start off low, when the property is relatively new, and then increase as it ages. These fees can be so high that they exceed the cost of simply renting a room at a nearby hotel for the same period of time.
- *Exchange problems*. It can be difficult to exchange your time slot and location for a different one, and doing so will probably require an extra fee. It may not be possible to secure a desired time slot or location at all, if it is at a busy resort.

- *Cost of debt.* Lenders do not like to lend money for the purchase of a timeshare. Those lenders that do offer mortgages will likely impose a higher-than-average interest rate.
- *Sale difficulty.* It is extremely difficult to sell a timeshare. Thousands of timeshare owners want to stop paying high maintenance fees, which has created an excess amount of timeshare supply, against which there is too little demand. The result is strong downward pressure on the prices at which timeshares can be sold. So many people want to sell their timeshares that there are consulting firms that charge a fee to assist in this process, or to help cancel a timeshare entirely.

Options for getting rid of a timeshare include gifting it to someone else, selling it at a significant loss, or renting out. A common option is to sell off a timeshare at a loss, just to avoid the ongoing maintenance fees.

In short, the only people who make money on timeshares are the developers who built and operate these properties. Investing in them is not advised.

> **Tip:** Avoid purchasing a fractionalized interest in *any* real estate; this is a common ploy by a developer to jack up the total price of a property by spreading the price among many investors.

Buy a Residential Property

There are several types of residential properties worth investing in. In the following bullet points, we note the key characteristics of each one:

- *Apartment buildings.* A particular advantage of owning an apartment building is that a majority of the units are generally rented out, so that some cash inflow can be expected in every month. On the other hand, there will be multiple tenants (and their problems) to deal with, which requires a relatively high level of oversight, and quite possibly the hiring of a property manager. These buildings tend to appreciate well over time, if they are properly maintained and located in a desirable neighborhood.
- *Single-family homes.* Single-family homes tend to appreciate in value faster than attached homes (such as townhouses), because there is more demand for this type of real estate. The main downside is that renting is an all-or-nothing proposition, where either the entire unit is rented or it stands empty.

> **Tip:** Only buy residential property in places where the cost to rent equals or exceeds the cost to own a home. When the cost to own exceeds the cost to rent, the market prices in the area are inflated.

- *Condominiums.* These are large property complexes that are comprised of individual units, each of which is owned separately. Ownership of one of these units means that you own the interior of a unit, as well as a proportionate interest in all common areas, such as the grounds and hallways. The home-owners' association actually owns and maintains the common areas, as well as the building structure. The maintenance costs tend to be lower for a condominium, since much of the exterior maintenance is handled by the home-owners' association – which benefits from volume purchases. A downside is that condominium demand tends to be lower than for single-family homes, so their market price appreciates at a slower rate.

Tip: Do not invest in condominiums located in older buildings, since they have aging plumbing, ventilation, and electrical systems that are in need of overhauls – and which result in very high assessments from the homeowners' association.

- *Cooperatives*. These are a form of shared housing in which each owner purchases a share of the entire building, which is represented by a stock certificate. The purchase gives you the right to inhabit a specific area within the building. The problem with cooperatives is that the association of homeowners must approve any remodeling plans and rental arrangements, and may even require the prior approval of a buyer. Given the severity of these restrictions, it is rarely a good idea to invest in a cooperative.

Flip a Residential Property

It is generally best to buy and hold residential property, in order to benefit from its appreciation in value over many years. An alternative approach is to buy and flip property. This strategy works best in hot markets where there is not enough available housing to meet demand, resulting in spiraling prices.

There are two ways to make money with the flipping strategy. One approach is to find a motivated seller (see the Ideal Seller section later in this chapter) who is willing to sell at a below-market price, and then immediately sell the property at full retail price. The other option is to buy a run-down property, make a number of judiciously-selected upgrades to maximize its price, and then sell it. In both cases, the intent is to sell the property quickly, in order to tie up capital for the minimum amount of time.

A key risk associated with flipping properties is transaction costs, which include inspection fees, closing costs, commissions, and title insurance. Another risk is that the cost of basic maintenance issues, as well as upgrade costs, turn out to be higher than expected, wiping out your anticipated profits. And yet another problem is the amount of time that a property will sit empty before it can be sold to a new buyer – during which it accrues mortgage interest costs, property taxes, utilities, homeowners' association dues, and so forth. A final concern is that the investor is not holding the property for very long, and so will pay ordinary income tax on any profit earned. In short, flipping properties is a risky strategy – despite the number of shows about this practice on television.

A further concern is that real estate prices might drop while the investor owns the property, so that its eventual sale is at a reduced price that might result in a loss. This scenario is more likely in a hot real estate market where lots of investors are piling in, hoping to flip their investments in short order for a profit. If a large number of these investors sense that the market is turning and sell off their properties, demand can dry up quickly, resulting in a sharp price decline. In this situation, the investor might be forced to retain ownership of the property for years, renting it out until prices return to a point at which it makes sense to sell.

In short, flipping property might initially sound like a good way to turn a profit within a short period of time, but this activity is impacted by so many risks that earning any reasonable amount of profit is actually quite difficult.

Buy Commercial Property

The commercial property classification is a broad one. It includes hotels, industrial, mobile home parks, offices, retail, self-storage, warehousing, and similar properties. Each of these property types requires significant expertise, so it makes sense to concentrate on one type in a specific area. By doing so, you can gain a better understanding of the quirks of the local market, and when there are pricing anomalies that can be exploited to generate above-average returns.

Investing in commercial property is an especially good idea when you can use some of the acquired space for your own business. By doing, you can avoid paying rent to a third party. In addition, being located on-site makes it easier to keep in touch with the other tenants, and learn about any problems they might be having with the facility.

There are several major concerns to be aware of when delving into commercial property investments. One is the risk that a property could have a high vacancy rate for an extended period of time. This can be caused by speculative construction in the area, as well as downturns in the economy that cool demand for office space. Another issue is that prospective tenants may demand costly upgrades to match their particular needs before they will agree to move in; this can represent a major cash outflow that may not be recovered from ongoing rent payments for several years. Alternatively, a prospective tenant may demand several months of free rent as part of a lease deal; this does not represent a cash outflow, but it does result in the absence of any cash inflows for a period of time. A final concern is that smaller tenants (which are your most likely pool of tenant candidates) are more likely to go out of business, leaving you with empty office space until a replacement can be found.

> **Tip:** Do not invest in commercial real estate when the supply of available space is increasing faster than the rate of demand for that space. This supply-demand imbalance will likely trigger a drop in lease rates.

Buy Undeveloped Land

A final possibility is to acquire undeveloped land. The strategy in doing so is to make the acquisition just before anyone else realizes that the land is about to be developed – perhaps to expand a nearby airport or to house a sports stadium. This is a dangerous approach, since the land does not generate any positive cash flow in the meantime, and you will have to at least pay property taxes on it every year. Furthermore, an investment in land that may not pay off for several years represents an opportunity cost, since the cash used to buy it could have been more profitably employed elsewhere. Also, lenders are less willing to issue mortgages on undeveloped land, since these loans are less likely to be paid off. To reduce their risk, lenders require a higher down payment, and will probably charge a higher interest rate. And to make things even more difficult, land cannot be depreciated, so there is no tax write-off associated with land investments.

The situation is quite different when the intent is to acquire undeveloped land, have it zoned for a particular type of real estate (such as residential housing) and then subdivide it into the authorized type of housing. Some investors sell out to property developers at this point, while others will engage in the construction process – though that requires forming a construction company to conduct the work.

Anyone investing in raw land should be aware of the following issues before doing so, in order to mitigate the risk of loss:

- *Monitor supply and demand.* Only acquire land in areas where there is robust demand for property, and especially when there is a shortage of available land.
- *Understand land access.* Have a clear understanding of the access rights to the property you want to acquire. If it is entirely landlocked, it may not be possible to acquire access, in which case the property is useless.
- *Understand the applicable zoning.* The local government will have zoned the property for a certain type of use. If you are contemplating a different type of development, and especially if local sentiments are against what you are proposing, then it is quite unlikely that the zoning will be altered to accommodate your wishes.
- *Understand cash outflows.* Be very clear about the tax, insurance, and other costs that will be incurred before you can sell the property to another party. Then estimate the longest period that you will likely need to hold it, and calculate the total cash outflow that you will incur during this period. Do you have sufficient cash reserves to sustain these losses?
- *Understand development costs.* When the intent is to develop the land to a certain extent before selling it to a developer, have a clear understanding of the costs that you will incur. This may involve expenditures for surveying, permits, and environmental studies – after which there will be payments for running utilities, installing stormwater controls, building roads, and so forth.

How to Acquire Real Estate

It always makes sense to acquire real estate for the lowest possible price, in order to achieve the highest possible gains thereafter. There are several ways to make below-market acquisitions, as we will detail in the following sub-sections.

Foreclosures

A *foreclosure* is the act of taking possession of a mortgaged property when the borrower fails to make scheduled mortgage payments. Once the lender has taken possession, it contracts with a local property management firm to prepare the property for sale. It then sells the property in order to generate enough cash to pay off the mortgage. The property sale is conducted at an auction, for which state laws have varying requirements for general notification – typically a posting in the local newspaper. Consider subscribing to one of the many local services that keep track of these notices, and which will forward them to you via email for a fee.

You can bid for these properties, and may score a below-market purchase. However, a number of large investment funds have also entered the business of buying foreclosed properties, and may outbid you or offer a package deal to the bank, buying a cluster of its foreclosed properties for cash. Another concern is that prospective bidders are rarely allowed to inspect a property prior to the auction, which presents the risk of learning about major problems only after you own it. A further issue is that 10% of the purchase price must usually be paid in cash at the auction, with the remainder due within 30 days; this can be a concern for a cash-strapped investor.

There are several points in the foreclosure process at which it is possible to acquire a property. Your options for profiting from the process vary, depending on which of these steps you choose to participate in. The options are as follows:

1. *Preforeclosure.* The preforeclosure period starts with the first time a homeowner misses a mortgage payment and extends through the notice of default filing by the lender. This is the point at which the borrower first begins to struggle with making payments. At this stage, it may be possible to approach the borrower with a buyout offer; accepting it will keep the borrower from having a foreclosure listed on his or her credit report, which may be tempting enough to allow for a low price being paid. This is an especially good option when you can make an all-cash offer, so that the borrower can walk away from the property in short order with some cash.

2. *Notice of default.* The next phase in the foreclosure process is when the lender files a notice of default. This triggers a multi-month process in which the lender gains the right to sell the property. At this point, the borrower is even more motivated to sell. However, the notice of default is accessible to the public, which means that other investors may possibly approach the buyer about a quick sale – which increases the level of competition, and therefore the price that will probably have to be paid to secure the property. A possible option here is to assume the borrower's mortgage, though this will be subject to the agreement of the lender, which will probably require a loan application and fee payment.

Tip: When buying from a borrower in the midst of a foreclosure, it can sometimes be difficult to remove the borrower from the premises. To ensure that this happens, only pay the borrower once he or she has vacated the premises.

3. *Foreclosure sale.* The next phase in the foreclosure process depends on the state. In a state that requires a judicial foreclosure, the lender must sue the borrower, which results in a court hearing where the court usually rules in

favor of the lender, allowing a sale to proceed. The lender then advertises the sale and hires a third party to conduct a public auction. In a state that does *not* require a lawsuit, the lender can proceed to a property sale more quickly. If those cases in which there is no bidder, the lender bids the outstanding amount of its loan, plus any penalties and fees, and takes possession of the property. You should set rules in advance of the bidding process, with a firm cap on how much you are willing to bid. Otherwise, you may end up with a property on which it is impossible to earn a profit. Or, if the lender ends up owning the property, it might be possible to negotiate a purchase immediately after the foreclosure sale, before the lender incurs any additional costs to start marketing the property for sale.

4. *Redemption period.* Some states permit a borrower to redeem property after a loan default has occurred, but before it has been foreclosed. Under these right of redemption rules, the borrower must pay back all the remaining principal, as well as any interest due and other costs incurred by the lender because of the default event. It may be possible to acquire the borrower's redemption rights, allowing you to make the required redemption payment and take possession of the property.

5. *Lender purchase.* In most cases, the lender will end up with title to a foreclosed property. When this happens, responsibility for the property is shifted to a department within the lender that dispositions these properties. It can make sense to learn about the procedures used by this department to sell off properties, which usually involves having local real estate brokers handle the sales work. The best way to acquire a property from a lender at this stage is to make an offer for a property that the lender would otherwise have to fix up before it can be ready for sale. The lender may be interested, if doing so can clear a nonperforming asset off its balance sheet in short order, and without consuming any more cash.

Tip: Do not begin to upgrade a property acquired at a foreclosure sale until the borrower's redemption period has ended. Otherwise, you will have invested in a property that is now owned by someone else.

Prior to making a bid, you should evaluate all structural problems and other maintenance issues with a property, itemizing the expenditures that will be needed to bring the property up a level at which it can be profitably rented. In addition, research whether there are any outstanding tax liens on the property. Based on this research, determine what your target price will be, and also establish a not-to-exceed bidding threshold. The threshold is mandatory – otherwise, there is a good chance that you will overbid in the heat of a competitive auction, and will then be burdened with an unprofitable investment.

Probate Sales

When a person dies, his or her estate enters a legal process known as probate. The probate process is overseen by a legal system administered by a probate court. When a deceased person owns real estate, it must be sold at the best possible price in order to maximize the value of the estate. The sale of this real estate is overseen by a probate court.

The court's first step is to authorized a real estate agent to list the property for sale. Next, the court sets a listing price, which is usually based on an appraisal and advice from the listing agent. At this point bidders can make an offer, which must be accompanied by a 10% down payment, usually in the form of a cashier's check. The estate representative is required to accept the highest bid, which will be made official after the court accepts the offer. During the court hearing, other bidders are allowed to make offers (called overbids[2]) that exceed the original offer. Also, family members of the decedent must be notified of the sale, and given time to comment on its terms.

A probate sale can be risky for an investor, especially because the rules about these sales vary by state. To ensure that you do not make any mistakes and possibly forfeit a down payment, be sure to work with a real estate agent and a real estate attorney during the process. Also, be sure to obtain a detailed inspection of the property prior to making an offer.

Despite these issues, many investors favor probate sales. This is because the more complicated sales process tends to drive away some bidders, resulting in less demand and therefore lower purchase prices. In addition, probate sales occur at all times, even during economic downturns when property owners are generally not willing to sell – which can result in lower purchase prices than would normally be obtained. And finally, probate sales can be considered an alternative property distribution channel, through which potentially high-value properties will be sold. In short, there are good reasons to keep tabs on probate sales in your area.

Short Sales

A *short sale* occurs when a homeowner sells his or her property to a third party for less than the amount due on the associated mortgage, with all proceeds going to the lender. This situation can be triggered when there is a decline in the value of real estate, so that borrowers have negative equity in their properties. It can also occur when a borrower has taken out a loan for more than the market value of the associated property, and is then unable to make the required payments. In both cases, if the borrower were to sell at the current market price, they would still owe money to the lender. For example, a homeowner has lost his job and the value of his house has declined, so he cannot make any additional payments on the $200,000 mortgage. Instead, he sells the property for $180,000, leaving a $20,000 deficiency that the lender agrees in advance to waive.

---

[2] Overbids are generally not allowed unless they exceed the current bid by at least five percent.

It may be possible for an investor to identify short-sale opportunities by subscribing to a service that tracks all notices of default issued by lenders. The trouble is, once a notice of default becomes public knowledge, other investors may contact the borrower as well, resulting in multiple offers to buy the property. If the borrower is interested in your proposal, the next step is to locate the person within the lender's bureaucracy who is empowered to deal with short sale proposals, which can be a difficult chore. All short sale paperwork should be sent to this person.

> **Note:** The original lender may have sold off its nonperforming mortgages to a third party for a discounted amount. Since the new loan holder paid less to acquire these mortgages, it may be more interested in accepting a short sale proposal – doing so allows it to convert a mortgage into cash, while still earning a profit.

Before the short sale process can begin, the lender must sign off on the decision to execute the sale. As part of this process, it will request documentation that clarifies why a short sale is being requested. The borrower will need to submit a financial package to the lender that proves his or her financial hardship, including financial statements, W-2 forms, payroll stubs, and bank statements. In addition, the listing agent sends the lender the buyer's purchase offer and a copy of the earnest money check. The submission package must be persuasive, since the lender will lose money on the transaction. Also, given the lender's loss, the process tends to be quite slow, and may take many months to complete. It is entirely possible that the lender will not accept the proposal; if it believes more money can be made through a standard foreclosure, then it may elect to take that approach instead.

> **Tip:** Have ready access to 100% of the cash needed to complete a short sale, perhaps through a pre-approved loan. Any lender that is about to take a loss on a short sale will only take cash to close the deal; it will not offer financing.

Despite the bureaucracy involved, borrowers in difficult circumstances may be amenable to a short sale, since this approach has a less negative impact on their credit rating. With a short sale, they can get out from under a mortgage they cannot afford, and no foreclosure appears on their credit report. In addition, they may be able to stay on the premises and rent from the new property owner.

The majority of short-sale properties are listed on the websites of real estate agents. These listings may not clearly identify a property as being a short sale transaction. Instead, look for wording that offers are subject to bank approval.

> **Note:** There is no borrower redemption requirement in a short sale, so investors do not have to worry about having the prior owner take back a property.

Acquisition Advisors

The process of finding, buying, operating, and selling property is quite time-consuming. Someone who successfully navigates this process is likely to be a detail-oriented person who is willing to investigate every aspect of a property before making a bid, and who is then willing to walk away if the proposed bid is rejected, rather than jacking up the offer to an unrealistic amount. This person is also willing to sort through dozens (if not hundreds) of properties in order to locate the best possible alternative, which calls for a great deal of patience.

In addition to these core attributes, a real estate investor also needs access to real estate knowledge concerning property inspections, tenants, property valuations, negotiations, and legal agreements. This calls for the formation of a small group of advisors who can jump in to assist on a new real estate project when needed. Having such a team is especially useful when trying to close a deal fast; having an expert on your side to evaluate a property inspection or draw up a sale agreement can spell the difference between buying the wrong property and getting the right one at a good price. This is especially important in a tight market, where there are lots of buyers and few sellers; being efficient in processing a transaction is more likely to result in a property purchase. Here are the key advisors to put on your team:

- *Appraiser*. A good appraiser has a detailed knowledge of local neighborhoods, and so can provide an expert opinion about which properties have the best upside potential, while also noting which upgrades will have the greatest impact on the market value of a property. The best appraisers are also aware of improvements being made by the local government (such as school expansions and new roads), and so have a good idea of which areas will be most favorably impacted by these changes.

- *Attorney*. A real estate attorney may not be needed for smaller property transactions, but it is advisable to retain one for larger transactions. This is because larger deals tend to be more complex. An attorney is especially useful on the front end of a transaction, drafting and reviewing the terms of a proposed deal. Their early participation is a good way to avoid major legal problems down the road.

- *Financial planner*. The goals to be achieved from real estate investing will vary, depending on your age and financial circumstances. For example, a younger investor might aggressively pursue increased cash flow in order to acquire more properties, while an older person facing retirement will be more concerned with the gradual sale of properties in order to harvest cash. A financial planner can provide advice about which types of investments make the most sense for you.

- *Lender*. Few real estate investors buy properties entirely with their own cash. Instead, they finance a large part of the total purchase price with a loan. When engaged in serial purchases, it can make sense to build a relationship with a local lender that specializes in your types of property investments, who can advise you in advance about whether you can qualify for a loan for a specific property. Also, having a relationship in place tends to accelerate the lending process. Note: In order to maintain a lending relationship, it is essential to always make loan payments on time for all existing mortgages; even a brief delay can shatter a lender's willingness to originate another mortgage.

- *Real estate agent*. It pays to have a qualified real estate agent working for you, handling real estate listings and transactions. The most-qualified agents work full-time, and specialize in the property types and geographic areas in which you want to invest. When you direct your business to one agent, that person is more likely to contact you first when the best opportunities come up, and before they are posted on an online listing service. They are also useful for negotiating the terms of a purchase or sale.

Tip: When evaluating a real estate agent, verify with the state licensing commission that the person has not been charged with any citations or disciplinary actions. If the person's license had been suspended or revoked at any time in the past, look elsewhere for an agent.

- *Taxation specialist*. The cash flow ultimately realized from real estate investing will be heavily impacted by the taxes paid on a property. A tax advisor can point out the advantages and disadvantages of various approaches to these investments, based on your specific financial situation. The advisor can also point out the documentation requirements for establishing your adjusted basis in a property. In particular, a tax advisor can be quite helpful when you want to sell property, since there are significant tax consequences associated with doing so.

A variation on obtaining the services of a real estate agent is to become one yourself. By doing so, you can avoid paying half of the commission that normally goes to an agent after a property sale has been completed. However, you will need to follow all local disclosure rules, so that the other parties to a transaction are aware that you are an agent.

Note: Be aware of when a real estate agent is working under a single agency or dual agency arrangement. Under a single agency arrangement, the agent is only representing one party – either the buyer or the seller. Under a dual agency arrangement, the agent (or two agents from the same firm) is representing both parties. The latter situation is a conflict of interest for the agent, so only work with an agent in a single agency relationship.

It can take time to assemble the perfect supporting cast. To do so, constantly evaluate your core group to see if they are actively assisting you, are good communicators, and will do whatever it takes to close a deal. If not, keep looking for better advisors.

Another consideration is how well you are supporting your advisors. A key consideration is that they will be more interested in working with you if you do not waste their time. This means only contacting them when you have a solid prospective property in hand, have the resources to acquire it, and will not waffle about closing a deal.

This advisory group can also send you important signals that you might be overpaying for a property. For example, a knowledgeable appraiser can tell you when the asking price of a property exceeds its actual value. Or, a lender that requires an unusually large down payment on a property is essentially saying that a property's price may be inflated. When these signals appear, it is time to back down from your offer price. There will always be other properties to bid on.

The Ideal Seller

When looking for a real estate investment that can be purchased at a below-market price, there are a few indicators to look for. One possibility is a seller who has been trying to sell for an extended period of time, without success. This situation may have arisen because the property is in poor shape, or there is no tenant. If the seller has waited for a sufficiently long time, it may be possible to take advantage of his frustration by offering an all-cash deal at a substantial discount.

A variation on the frustrated seller concept is to buy from someone who has been managing multiple properties for a long time, and who now wants to exit the business – or at least have fewer properties to manage. This individual is probably more aware of market prices (being a real estate investor), so the odds of obtaining a massive price reduction are not great. Nonetheless, it may be possible to use the person's annoyance with the situation to chip away at the owner's target price.

Another example of an ideal seller is a person who is moving – perhaps at the behest of an employer – and who needs to sell her current property in order to have enough cash to buy a property in the new location. This is a time-sensitive situation, so if you can swoop in with a somewhat below-market offer, it may be possible to secure a deal on a quality property.

A variation on the preceding situation is when a person is motivated to sell for any reasons other than moving out of the area. This individual might have to move due to an unexpected illness (such as moving in with a sick parent), a divorce, or being laid off from a job. In this case, the owner needs to downsize quickly, and so may be interested in accepting a reduced offer in exchange for a fast close.

While these situations sound like golden opportunities for a real estate investor, you have to *find* them. This requires a high degree of networking through the community, in order to hear about them before any other investors do. It can make sense to be on particularly good terms with local real estate agents, who are in a position to hear about these situations first.

Like-Kind Exchanges

It is possible for a real estate investor to engage in a tax-free exchange of property. This can be done when the property given up is similar to the property obtained, and the property is to be held for productive use in business or as an investment (these exchanges do not apply to residential property). While such an exchange does not result in an immediate tax liability, it does carry forward any unrecognized gain or loss that might otherwise have been recognized by carrying forward the owner's adjusted basis into the replacement property. The owner will eventually recognize this gain or loss when the replacement property is sold.

To qualify for like-kind exchange treatment, the property to be exchanged must be identified within 45 days and the exchange must be finalized within 180 days. If these time periods cannot be observed, then the transaction becomes a taxable sale.

Note: A like-kind exchange does not require that the respective properties be identical, only that they have a similar nature or character. The properties do not have to be of the same quality.

Any money received in addition to a like-kind property will trigger the recognition of a gain, but only to the extent of the cash received.

EXAMPLE

A real estate investor exchanges a medical office building worth $2 million and with an adjusted basis of $1.8 million for a similar building worth $2.1 million. The taxpayer pays the other party $100,000 in addition to the property given up. The taxpayer's basis for the building received is $1.9 million (calculated as $1.8 million adjusted basis + $100,000 cash paid).

The taxpayer on the other side of the transaction has an adjusted basis of $1.5 million in her property, so she has an unrecognized gain of $600,000 (the difference between the market value of her property and the adjusted basis). She only recognizes this gain to the extent of the cash received, which is $100,000.

When one party to an exchange takes on liabilities associated with an exchanged property, the amount of the mortgage is considered to be money received by the party trading away the liability. When there is a mortgage associated with both properties being exchanged, only a net reduction in mortgage debt is considered to be cash received.

EXAMPLE

Mr. Smith owns a building with an adjusted basis of $600,000, and which is subject to a mortgage of $100,000. Mr. Smith transfers the building to Mr. Jones in exchange for $30,000 in cash and a similar building with a fair value of $700,000. Mr. Jones takes on the mortgage previously held by Mr. Smith. As a result of this exchange, Mr. Smith realizes a gain of $230,000, which is computed as follows:

Value of property received	$700,000
Cash received	30,000
Mortgage transferred	100,000
Amount realized	$830,000
Minus: Basis of transferred property	600,000
Gain realized	$230,000

The taxable amount of the realized gain is $130,000, which is the amount of the cash received and the mortgage transferred to Mr. Jones.

Any commissions and other payments made as part of a property exchange reduces any gain on the transaction. These amounts are also added to the basis of the property received. For example, if the commission associated with the exchange in the preceding example had been $5,000, then Mr. Smith's realized gain would have been $225,000 instead of $230,000. It also would have increased his adjusted basis from $600,000 to $605,000.

Installment Sales

Usually, the buyer of a property pays the seller in full, either directly in cash or with a mortgage obtained from a third party. Sometimes, however, the seller provides the buyer with financing, in which case the buyer makes a series of payments to the seller over a period of time. If this arrangement qualifies as an installment sale, then the seller can incrementally report gains from the sale upon the receipt of each individual payment. This arrangement is allowed by the tax code so that sellers providing financing do not have to report the entire amount of a gain at the point of sale without having actually received payment in full from the buyer. A further benefit for the seller is that a series of partial gains recognized over multiple tax years may put the seller in a lower tax bracket, resulting in a lower overall tax. However, a seller may elect out of an installment sale arrangement when it wants to recognize the entire amount of a gain at the point of sale, perhaps because there is a loss to offset, or tax rates are expected to rise in the future.

A sales arrangement qualifies as an installment sale when at least one payment will be received in a later tax year. However, installment sales treatment is not allowed when a loss will result from the sale of property; in this case, the full amount of the loss must be reported in the year of sale.

When receiving payments under an installment sales arrangement, the seller reports as income that portion of the payments received that comprise a gain from the sale, as well as the interest income associated with the loan extended to the buyer. The amount of gain is reported ratably as each payment is received from the buyer. The gain reported is derived by multiplying the amount of each payment by the gross profit ratio, which is the ratio of the total gross profit[3] to be realized to the total contract price.

---

[3] Gross profit is the selling price of a property minus its adjusted basis. Interest is not included in the selling price.

EXAMPLE

Mr. Johnson sells a property to Ms. White for $250,000, where Ms. White pays $50,000 down and the remainder is payable in equal annual installments over the next five years, plus a sufficient amount of interest. Mr. Johnson's basis in the property is $180,000. The selling expenses that he pays are $5,000.

The gross profit on the sale is $65,000, which is calculated as the $250,000 sale price, minus the $180,000 basis and $5,000 of selling expenses. The gross profit ratio is 26%, which is calculated as the gross profit of $65,000 divided by the $250,000 sale price. Therefore, $10,400 of each annual $40,000 payment is a gain on the sale. Mr. Johnson must also report the interest received each year as ordinary interest income.

A few additional rules pertaining to installment sales are as follows:

- *Mortgage implications.* If the buyer under an installment arrangement takes on a property that is subject to a mortgage, taking on the mortgage is not considered a payment.
- *Subsequent price reduction.* If the parties later agree to a reduced selling price, this will alter the gross profit on the sale. When this happens, the gross profit ratio is only adjusted on remaining payments; there is no adjustment to the gain reported in earlier years.
- *Tradable obligations.* When the seller can readily convert a buyer's obligation to pay into cash, this constitutes constructive receipt of the cash, and so triggers reporting of the related amount of gain. This is usually the case only when the obligation is in the form of a registered bond that can be traded in a securities market (a rare circumstance). If the obligation is converted to cash, then there may be a gain or loss associated with the sale of the obligation.
- *Unstated interest.* If the sales agreement does not provide that the buyer will pay a stated amount of interest, then a part of each payment due after the first six months must include an interest component. This imputed interest is calculated according to the most recent IRS formulation and reduces the selling price, which in turn reduces the calculated gain.

Real Estate Investment Best Practices

There are several ways to improve the returns from your real estate investments. The following best practices apply to all aspects of the process of searching for, acquiring, operating, and selling real estate:

- *Buy in built-out areas.* Property values tend to hold up better in areas where there is minimal undeveloped land, because no additional units can be built.
- *Buy where property is owner-occupied.* Neighborhoods are more stable when a large proportion of the properties are occupied by their owners. This tends to increase property values, so try to purchase rental properties in these areas.

- *Look for high cost-benefit upgrades.* When searching for property, look for fixes that are relatively easy and inexpensive to complete, and for which tenants will be willing to tolerate a significant rent increase. Examples of these fixes are a new coat of paint, new flooring, modest landscaping improvements, and new hardware on cabinets and drawers.
- *Avoid properties with significant deferred maintenance.* When the current owner of a property has clearly deferred major maintenance on a building (such as replacing a roof), it is a good bet that other undisclosed maintenance must also be completed – which will eat up your cash reserves. These properties should be avoided, even if the owner appears willing to accept a low price.
- *Avoid buying converted apartments.* Developers sometimes convert older apartment buildings into condominiums and then sell the units. While the fit and finish of these units might look quite nice, the underlying structure of the building is old and probably in need of a substantial amount of maintenance – which triggers ongoing increases in the assessments charged to the property owners. They also tend to have poor sound proofing, which will annoy your tenants and increase their turnover rate.
- *Avoid scattered properties.* It can be quite difficult to personally manage a number of smaller properties scattered over a wide area, especially when these properties are in need of ongoing maintenance. A better approach is to concentrate your investing in a small number of larger properties, with professional on-site management.
- *Avoid distant investment areas.* Some parts of the country have occasionally been tagged as being hot real estate markets. Recent examples are Miami and Phoenix. If you do not live in these areas, it is not prudent to invest there, because you do not know the details of the market. It is generally better to concentrate on regions with which you have a greater degree of familiarity.
- *Review foreclosed properties extra carefully.* When a property owner walks away from a property, leaving it for the lender, there is a fair chance that the person did so because there were severe problems that would cost more to remediate than their equity in the property (such as asbestos remediation or a cracked slab). There may also be liens against the property. Yet another possibility is the absence of permits on changes made to the property. All of these issues can cost significant amounts to remediate. Consequently, be extra careful about reviewing foreclosed properties before submitting a bid to buy them.
- *Adopt a rent-raising strategy.* Do not impose large rent increases at one time, because it can trigger a tenant exodus. Instead, consider a series of incremental increases, which existing tenants are more likely to tolerate. Also, consider whether any cost-effective improvements to the property can justify a rent increase, such as updates to kitchens, bathrooms, common areas, and elevators.
- *Minimize tenant turnover.* Profits can be severely impacted when units remain empty after a tenant leaves. You will also have to expend significant amounts to advertise for new tenants, screen them, and pay commissions. To minimize

tenant turnover, be highly responsive to tenant needs, keep the property in pristine condition, and encourage tenants to sign longer-term leases.

- *Replace marginal tenants.* Though we just advised you to retain your current tenants, this does not apply to your worst tenants – those who bother their neighbors, complain constantly, and damage the building. In these cases, view the end of their lease agreements as an opportunity not to renew, so that you can search for higher-quality tenants.

- *Emphasize curb appeal.* A good way to attract new tenants is to clean up the exterior of the property and ensure that it always looks better than the surrounding properties, perhaps by improving the landscaping. Getting interested prospects to enter the building is the first step in keeping the property full of tenants.

- *Look for cost reductions.* There may be ways to cut back on expenses in ways that do not impact the look of the property, and which tenants will not care about. For example, a drip irrigation system can reduce the cost of water, while an energy audit may highlight the possibility of using LED lighting or adding insulation to cut electricity costs. Or, consider aggregating your insurance needs for several properties into one policy, which can cut your total insurance cost.

- *Refinance the property.* Watch mortgage rates, and consider refinancing at a lower interest rate if rates fall sufficiently to offset the cost of the financing fees. Further, consider refinancing using a shorter mortgage term, such as 15 years, since these arrangements require much smaller interest payments in aggregate (though the monthly mortgage bill will be larger). Another possibility is to pay extra whenever you have some excess cash, which reduces the term of the mortgage and therefore the aggregate amount of interest paid.

- *Be ready to sell.* Regularly review the direction in which prices are going in the area surrounding your property, and be willing to sell if it appears that local conditions are causing your property to depreciate in value. For example, an increase in the crime rate can cause a sharp decline in local values. In these cases, it may be better to sell now, thereby freeing up the cash to purchase property elsewhere, where there is a better chance of appreciation. The overall strategy should be to shift from less desirable areas into more desirable ones in order to enhance your opportunities for property appreciation.

Summary

Real estate investing can be quite profitable. However, go back and read through the How to Acquire Real Estate section in this chapter. The narrative contains many comments about the large number of other investors who are also in the market, looking for the next great deal. In addition, do not count on hoodwinking an owner into selling a foreclosed property at a deep discount to the market price; owners are generally sophisticated, with a good knowledge of the value of their real estate holdings, and sufficient connections with real estate agents to sell their properties for close to the market price. In short, it can be difficult to acquire real estate for a great price. Your focus should be more on not paying more than the market price, and then relying on good operational skills and property appreciation to earn a profit over the long term.

Chapter 2
Property Financing

Introduction

It requires a substantial amount of cash to purchase real estate, which can make it difficult to become an investor in this area. In this chapter, we review a number of techniques for obtaining the financing needed to invest in real estate. But first, we address the issue of what an active real estate investing lifestyle will do to your investment mix.

Asset Allocation Issues

Before investing in real estate, consider your mix of equity and debt investments. Investment advisors generally recommend that a younger person invest primarily in equity securities, since doing so tends to generate a higher return on investment. Then, as a person ages, the recommended investment mix trends toward more debt investments, such as bonds. This shift in strategy is intended to move funds into less-variable investments, so that cash will be available when a person eventually retires.

The asset allocation mix can become an issue when you invest heavily in real estate, because this is an equity investment. It tends to have a higher return on investment, but the outcome can vary substantially over time, depending on cash inflows from tenants and changes in the market value of a property. Consequently, consider scaling back on your real estate investments as you approach retirement age, selling off properties when their market values are high, and shifting the resulting cash into less variable investments. Conversely, it may be entirely acceptable to invest heavily in real estate when you are younger and care less about short-term variations in property valuations; in this case, your focus is on aggressively growing both the cash flows and valuations of your investment properties.

Your Personal Credit

Investing in real estate is likely to be the single largest investment you will make in your life. There is a risk that, if you acquire property with all of your cash, plus a mortgage obligation, you will be caught wrong-footed if there is an economic decline within the next few years that drives away tenants or reduces the value of the property. To mitigate this risk, review your personal expenses prior to making any investments, and see if anything can be pruned away. This means eliminating all high-interest-rate consumer debt, expensive vacations, and replacements of major assets (such as cars) that are not yet entirely worn out. The resulting spartan spending habits will allow you to generate more cash to offset any shortfalls associated with the real estate investments.

Tip: There are two ways to save money. The traditional approach is to cut your expenses, while the other option is to raise your income. The cutting expenses option has a finite cap on how much money you can save, since you cannot save more than your income. The raising income option has no such limitation, since your income can be raised by several hundred percent (or more). Therefore, when selecting a career path, take a hard look at the potential earnings to be achieved. You can invest in far more real estate when you are (for example) a doctor than if you are a bricklayer.

It will not be necessary to maintain a high level of penury for an extended period of time – after all, what is the point of becoming a real estate investor if you cannot enjoy the proceeds? Instead, assume a thrifty attitude for the first few years, until you have built up a decent cash reserve that can handle the worst declines in cash inflows that you are likely to experience.

Besides reducing your expenses, another necessary task is to improve your credit score to the greatest extent possible. Lenders will only agree to a mortgage if you have established a sterling record of paying on time, every time. To this end, obtain a copy of your personal credit report, identify any issues that are dragging down your score, and remediate them before applying for a mortgage. If these issues are still on your credit report at the time of a loan application, then address them up-front with the lender, to explain your side of the situation. This is also useful for pruning out those lenders for which you might otherwise spend a great deal of time filling out loan application forms, only to be rejected over the credit report issue.

Tip: You will qualify for a larger mortgage if you have less consumer debt, so pay off your car loans and credit card debt before applying for a mortgage.

The Need for Cash

The vast majority of all real estate deals will require some amount of up-front cash payment. There may be a few marginal properties on the market that can be acquired for no money down, but these are rare – and will probably require substantial maintenance investments to bring them up to a tolerable standard. There may also be a few cases in which a loan can be obtained for more than the market value of a property, but the associated loan repayment obligations make these arrangements risky. Furthermore, the most high-grade investment properties all require a cash down payment. Consequently, it is nonsensical to attempt investing in real estate without any initial cash.

That being said, where is the cash supposed to come from in order to purchase a property? The traditional arrangement is for an investor to pay a moderate cash amount as a down payment, and finance the remainder with a mortgage on the property. The amount of cash needed will depend on the requirements of the lender, but the best interest rates can generally only be obtained when the down payment is at least 25% of the purchase price. If you can only manage a lower down payment, then expect the resulting mortgage to have an associated interest rate that is several percent higher. The higher rate can have a profound effect on the size of the monthly mortgage payment, possibly resulting in an investment that turns out to have a negative return, especially during the early years of the arrangement.

EXAMPLE

Sarah wants to purchase a $500,000 residential property, which she intends to rent out. A lender mandates that she must pay a 25% down payment, which is $125,000. She will also need to pay 5% of the purchase price in closing costs, which is another $25,000. This means that Sarah will need to come up with a cash payment of $150,000 in order to obtain a mortgage of $375,000 that will cover the remainder of the purchase price.

Options for Obtaining a Down Payment

There are multiple options available for obtaining a down payment, besides the basic approach of saving up for it. We note the options in the following bullet points:

- *Make a lower down payment.* Though a 25% down payment is optimal for reducing interest costs, it may be possible to make a substantially smaller down payment. Doing so will result in higher interest costs, and the lender will likely require that you also pay for private mortgage insurance (which protects the lender in the event of a default).
- *Buy a cheaper property.* Your savings may not be sufficient for a 25% down payment on a $1,000,000 property, but they might be fine if you set your sights lower and buy a lower-cost property. If you have saved $100,000, that will be well below the optimal down payment for the $1,000,000 property, but will be fine for a $400,000 property.
- *Rent out space.* It may be possible to use your smaller down payment to move into a somewhat larger residential property, and then rent out space in it. The resulting rental payments will help you to gradually build up more cash for a larger purchase at some point in the future.
- *Refinance.* If you already own a home on which the associated mortgage is at a relatively high interest rate and current mortgage rates are lower, consider refinancing it at the current rate. Doing so should result in lower monthly payments (depending on the duration of the new mortgage), which frees up more cash that can be put towards a down payment.
- *Take out a home equity loan.* A lesser option than refinancing your home is to take out a home equity loan on it. This is not as good an option, because you must now make a second monthly payment, in addition to the mortgage payment – which increases the risk of default. In addition, lenders consider these loans to be riskier, and so charge a higher interest rate on them. Nonetheless, a home equity loan can provide a substantial amount of additional cash.
- *Ask for seller financing.* Some sellers will be amenable to offering financing, sometimes allowing only a modest down payment. This situation may arise when the seller already has lots of cash in the bank, and would prefer to

receive payments over an extended period of time (which reduces their taxable income). However, these situations usually come with a caveat, which is that the seller was unable to sell the property by any other means. Consequently, in these situations, review the property especially hard for flaws, such as expensive maintenance problems. When a property has been on the market for a long time and seller financing is being offered, it is a good bet that there are problems with the property.

- *Find another investor*. If you absolutely *must* purchase an especially expensive property, consider bringing in another investor who has enough cash to make up your down payment shortfall. This approach is especially useful when a property will require significant upgrades for which you do not have enough cash. Be sure to thoroughly document the arrangement, since an acrimonious relationship can be expensive.
- *Find a cosigner*. A family member (typically a parent) may be in a comfortable enough situation to agree to be a consigner on a loan. In this case, the lender is more likely to make its lending decision based on the financial statements of the cosigner. Of course, a foreclosure represents a significant risk to the cosigner, so be sure to fully discuss the consequences of cosigning.

Tip: Partnering with another investor will only work if you are compatible, so spend time up front exploring the other person's expectations for a prospective investment, including who is responsible for maintenance, what to do if/when more cash is required, and how long he or she wants to park cash in the investment property. This investigation may reveal that the other partner would be a bad fit, in which case it is better not to invest at all.

When reviewing the preceding options, the key issue to remember is that taking out more loans on an existing property presents the risk of being overleveraged, where you have more debt than you can pay off. This can result in the foreclosure of your existing home. A better approach is to wait and pile up more cash before making a down payment – and even then, have some extra cash on hand in case your financial situation turns out to be less than optimal.

Mortgage Options

There are two types of mortgages – fixed rate and variable rate. As the name implies, a *fixed-rate mortgage* has an interest rate associated with it that remains constant over the entire term of the mortgage. The key advantage of a fixed-rate mortgage is that the size of every mortgage payment is fixed over the entire term of the loan, so there is no uncertainty about how much must be paid each month. However, this rate is typically higher than the initial rate offered on a variable-rate mortgage, so the interest paid will probably be higher for a fixed-rate mortgage over the short term. This is a major consideration when your intent is to buy a property, fix it up, and then sell it off after a short period of time; in this case, a variable-rate mortgage is a better option. Another concern is that interest rates could drop after you have locked in a fixed interest rate, in which case you may find it necessary to refinance at the new, lower interest rate – which can be expensive. And if you do want to refinance, some fixed-rate mortgages have prepayment penalties that make it too expensive to refinance. In short, the fixed-rate option is a good one when the intent is to hold onto a property for a long time, while it is a less viable option for shorter-term ownership situations.

An *adjustable-rate mortgage* has an interest rate that can change over time. The initial rate offered (the teaser rate) is usually quite low – less than the rate for a fixed-rate mortgage – and is then adjusted at fixed intervals (usually every six or 12 months) over the course of the mortgage to track the current mortgage rate. This structure works well when you do not intend to keep a property for long, so that you can take advantage of the low initial rate and not have to worry about subsequent changes. It is also a good choice when you expect mortgage rates to decline over time, since the mortgage rate will decline along with the market rate. However, there are several downsides to a variable-rate mortgage. First, the initial rate is set quite low in order to attract borrowers, after which the rate will increase – perhaps by so much that the arrangement results in negative cash flows from a property. Second, the formula for determining the future interest rate on the mortgage could be highly unfavorable to the borrower, typically involving a fixed margin (such as 3%) that is tacked on to an index value (such as the rate on a one-year Treasury Bill)[4].

The specific index used to calculate the interest rate on a variable-rate mortgage can have a profound impact on the speed with which the rate increases. Some indexes respond quite rapidly to changes in interest rates, which means that the interest rate can spike quite suddenly. However, the mortgage agreement may cap the size of interest rate increases over a certain period of time, so that the effect of any rate spikes is spread out over a longer period of time. For example, interest rate changes may be capped (up or down) at 1% per year. In addition, these mortgage agreements contain a lifetime cap on the grand total amount by which the interest rate can be increased over the life of a mortgage; a typical lifetime cap is 5% over the initial teaser rate. This cap also applies in the reverse direction, so that the interest rate will never decline below the initial teaser rate.

Tip: Calculate the maximum monthly mortgage that you would pay at the highest possible variable rate allowed under a prospective mortgage agreement. If this rate will result in negative cash flows, use a fixed-rate mortgage instead.

Tip: Search through the loan documentation for a variable-rate mortgage to find the margin and index value that are used to derive the future interest rate. You can use this information to determine what the interest rate is likely to be once the initial period for the teaser rate is over.

---

[4] Some of the indexes used to derive the interest rates on variable-rate mortgages are Treasury Bills, Treasury Notes, and certificates of deposit.

> **Tip:** You can negotiate with a lender to cap the rate at which a variable-rate mortgage can increase the interest rate charged, though it will usually require a higher initial rate or the payment of more points.

An analysis of the interest rate formula on a variable-rate mortgage may reveal that its rate is actually quite similar to that of a fixed-rate mortgage. If so, the fixed-rate mortgage is the better deal, since it contains no risk that the rate will increase further.

A pernicious form of variable-rate mortgage to be wary of is when the maximum monthly mortgage payment is capped, but the maximum interest rate is not. In this case, you can end up paying less than the total interest due each month, which means that the unpaid interest is added to the loan principal. In effect, the size of the mortgage increases over time. This situation is referred to as *negative amortization*. When negotiating with a lender, be sure to ask if this situation exists in proposed mortgage terms. If you agree to such terms, be aware that the only way to get out from under the increasing principal balance on the mortgage is to eventually sell the associated property for a substantially higher price than you paid for it.

Another loan option is the *balloon loan*, where the entire principal balance is paid off as of a specific date. This means that you are only paying the interest on the loan until its repayment date, which can make the cash flows from the property look quite acceptable. The downside of this arrangement is, of course, that the principal must eventually be paid in a lump sum. If it is not possible to refinance as the repayment date approaches, the lender will be able to foreclose on the property. Given this concern, only resort to a balloon loan when no other options are available and you absolutely, positively must own the property for which it is intended. If you do elect to take the balloon loan option, then take one with the longest possible due date; this gives you more time to figure out a refinancing option.

> **Tip:** If the only way to invest in a property is to buy it with a balloon loan, it probably means that the associated cash flows will be marginal for an extended period of time. When this is the case, the more prudent approach is to not buy the property at all; something else with more favorable cash flows will eventually come along.

Mortgage Fees

A lender can and will charge a number of fees when it originates a mortgage. You should review the lending paperwork in advance to ascertain the size and validity of these charges; some may be negotiable. We describe these fees in the following subsections.

When selecting a lender, it can be useful to ask each lender under consideration for a list of their fees, so that you can compare them and spot any pricing anomalies. A variation on the concept is to obtain seller financing; sellers offering financing may not charge any of these fees, because their loan approval process is much simpler than what a bank would use.

Application Fee

Lenders usually charge an application fee, which covers the cost of processing a loan application. This fee is usually a few hundred dollars. Watch out for an inordinately large fee, such as $1,000.

Appraisal Fee

Lenders will hire an appraiser to develop an estimate of the value of the property to be acquired. They need this information in order to keep from lending more money than the property is worth. Otherwise, if the borrower defaults, the lender will not be able to recover its loaned funds by foreclosing on and selling the property. The cost of this appraisal varies, depending on the size of the property. Residential unit appraisals are in the hundreds of dollars, while the appraisal of a larger commercial property could run into the thousands.

Credit Report Fee

Lenders may charge through their cost to obtain your credit report. A *credit report* is a detailed breakdown of a person's credit history that is prepared by a credit bureau. A lender needs to review this report to see if a mortgage applicant has had any credit problems in the past, such as late payments or a bankruptcy. The fee charged should be well under $100.

Environmental Assessment Fee

Lenders will pay an engineering firm to conduct an environmental assessment of larger commercial properties. These assessments can include a review of issues in the surrounding area. Environmental assessment fees vary dramatically based on the location, but can run well over $10,000.

Inspection Fee

Lenders will require an inspection of any property for which they will be providing a mortgage. This inspection is needed to spot major issues, such as termite damage or structural flaws. The average cost of a home inspection is about $500, with inspections costing much more for larger commercial properties.

Points

When issuing a mortgage, a lender charges an up-front fee, called *points*. The amount of the levy is usually a percentage of the total amount borrowed. For example, 2 points on a $250,000 mortgage is $5,000. This charge can be characterized as prepaid interest.

The amount paid for points on a mortgage is a particular concern when you only plan to keep a property for a short period of time, or if you have minimal cash available. In this case, it makes sense to lower the points as much as possible. This can be achieved by accepting a higher interest rate on the mortgage, where the payment for points is essentially being deferred into the future. Conversely, when you have excess cash right now and plan to hold onto a property for an extended period of time, consider offering to trade more points now for a lower interest rate on the mortgage. Doing so increases the monthly cash flow that the property will spin off.

Tip: To compare the interest rates being offered by various lenders, ask for a quote using the same baseline number of points, such as two points.

When a lender offers a loan with no points, this only means that the lender has transferred the cost into the interest rate being charged, which will be higher than the market rate. If the proposed interest rate seems reasonable, review the lender's other fees – it is making up for the lack of points *somewhere* in its fee structure.

Mortgage Duration

The typical duration of a mortgage is 30 years, with many lenders also offering 15-year terms. It may be possible to arrange for some other mortgage length, but these are the standard mortgage durations. It might initially make sense to acquire a 15-year loan, since the associated interest rate is somewhat lower, resulting in a reduced overall lending cost. However, compressing the mortgage term in this manner also increases the size of the monthly mortgage payment substantially. This increase in the monthly payment could put investors at risk of foreclosure, especially if the returns from a property are expected to be quite minimal. To reduce the risk of foreclosure, it can make more sense to obtain a 30-year mortgage, thereby minimizing the monthly mortgage payments.

A low-risk option is to select a 30-year mortgage, and then make additional payments on it if you have sufficient cash flow to do so. If not, just make the normal payments. This approach will reduce the time required to pay off the mortgage, while minimizing the risk of a foreclosure. Of course, this option only works if the lender does not charge a fee for prepayments.

Finding a Lender

There are many lenders from which to choose, if you have a great credit rating and a large down payment. If not, finding a lender can be a bit more difficult. There are several ways to find one. First, try to obtain a referral from someone else in the real estate field, such as your real estate agent, tax advisor, or financial planner. These people may be able to arrange an introduction. Another option is to ask other investors who are working in the same geographic area. These contacts should be able to provide you with connections to the best lenders in the area for the types of properties you want to acquire.

Referrals are not just necessary for when your credit credentials are somewhat questionable. The reverse situation arises when your credentials *are* first rate. Lenders you have never heard of may make contact, soliciting your business. It pays to be suspicious in these cases, so explore their references. An unsolicited lender may offer uncompetitive terms, hoping that you will not read the fine print or explore the extent of the additional fees being charged.

It is usually sufficient to work directly with a lender for a smaller, straightforward mortgage. These are for lower-priced residential properties in good locations and with few maintenance issues. For more complex or questionable deals, your only choice may be to work through a mortgage broker, who will conduct a search on your behalf with a variety of lender contacts. Brokers can be quite useful when a broad range of terms are being offered by multiple lenders, and you need assistance in sorting through them to determine the best option. They are also useful for completing the application forms demanded by lenders (which is especially useful if you are not an organized person). Mortgage brokers work on a commission basis, so it pays to expend some effort sourcing funding by yourself, before falling back on this option.

> **Note:** Mortgage brokers are not cheap. They generally charge between one and two percent of the funding amount, though this percentage declines for larger mortgages.

> **Tip:** If you plan to use a mortgage broker, check their references first. Some use bait-and-switch tactics, where they initially promise a great deal and then backtrack on the basis of some perceived flaw in your loan package, such as your credit report. Other people who have worked with the broker can give you a better view of the broker's honesty.

Recourse and Nonrecourse Financing

The prudent investor will certainly have an interest in minimizing the risk associated with a mortgage. One way to do this is to only accept *nonrecourse* financing, where the lender cannot pursue the investor's personal assets for repayment; instead, foreclosing on the associated property is the only way for the lender to obtain repayment of the amount outstanding. Only dealing with nonrecourse financing prevents a catastrophic loss on any one property from damaging your personal assets. Given the increased risk to the lender in this situation, expect the lender to only agree to a significantly smaller mortgage amount. This is definitely the preferred option for investors.

The reverse situation is a *recourse* loan, where the lender can pursue an investor's personal assets for repayment of a mortgage. The only case in which it makes sense to accept a recourse loan is when there are no other financing options – which usually means that lenders do not believe that the property in question is a viable investment opportunity. It may have significant maintenance issues, or has an unusually high vacancy rate. If so, consider whether you really want to accept the downside risk associated with the property failing – you could lose your personal assets, including your home.

A variation on the recourse loan concept is the loan guarantee. A lender may insist that the investor wanting to purchase a property provide a personal guarantee that the loan will be repaid. If so, a reasonable pushback is to only accept the guarantee if there is a cap on its amount; doing so limits the investor's potential losses.

Your Personal Financial Statement

Any lender you approach about a property mortgage will want to see your personal financial statement, to see if you have sufficient net worth to make mortgage payments. This statement lists your assets, liabilities, income, and expenses. In the following sub-sections, we provide examples of what each element of your personal financial statement should contain. It also helps to assemble a set of explanations for any issues that appear on the personal financial statement. For example, if expenses were unusually high last year, you could explain that a medical emergency in the family caused a one-time spike in medical bills, and also note what your profits would have been without this unexpected expense.

Assets

A listing of assets should contain everything of significance that you own. The exact threshold below which assets may be ignored will depend on the circumstances. Start with a high threshold – perhaps $25,000 – to see how many assets appear on the list, and then reduce the threshold if the list is excessively skimpy. Also, list even those assets for which there is an associated debt; the debt will appear in the liabilities section of the personal financial statement. Finally, list the current market value of each asset, rather than the price at which it was originally acquired. This is especially important for a house, where the market value could be far different from the purchase price. The following exhibit contains a sample asset listing, including a description of the types of assets that should be included.

Sample Personal Financial Statement: Assets Listing

Cash and Cash Equivalents: This is the current cash balance in every financial account held. It may include funds held in a savings bank, credit union, or other financial services entity, as well as loose cash kept in the house.	
Checking account (#12345678-001) at Third Pacific Bank	$34,200
Savings account (#87654321-023) at Second Atlantic Bank	42,800
Subtotal	$77,000
Marketable Securities: This is the current market value of all publicly-traded stocks, bonds, and mutual funds owned. The market value of stocks is derived from their most recent bid price.	
Amalgamated Concrete (20,000 shares)	$39,000
Barbeque Industries (18,000 shares)	71,000
Subtotal	$110,000
Accounts Receivable: This is all loans owed to you by other parties. State only the unpaid balance, as well as any property used as security.	
Albert Ellingwood (friend; unsecured note; payable in monthly installments)	$18,000
Carl Blaurock (friend; unsecured note; payable in monthly installments)	9,000
Subtotal	$27,000
Cash Value of Life Insurance: This is the current cash surrender value of a whole life insurance policy. This amount can be obtained from the insurance agent that sold you the policy.	
Greater Bahamas Life Company (whole life policy #750152-71	$24,000
Subtotal	$24,000
Real Estate: This is all real estate you own, noting the address. An on-line real estate valuation estimate can be used for the market value.	
Personal residence (3,500 square feet, at 123 East Main Street, Boulder CO)	$1,750,000
Vacation home (1,700 square feet 2-bedroom condo, 48 Skyview Lane, Steamboat CO)	900,000
Subtotal	$2,650,000
Personal Property: This is all assets owned other than real estate. More expensive items should be listed separately, and everything else in a single aggregated line item. It may be necessary to obtain an appraisal for jewelry, artwork, and antiques.	
Chevrolet pickup truck	$31,000
Wellcraft bass boat	82,000
Subtotal	$113,000

Other Assets: This is a catchall for all other assets, including unlisted securities, IRAs, vested pension plans, and interests in other businesses.	
Acme Speedboats (unlisted company; 2,500 shares)	$30,000
Vested pension plan	$84,000
Subtotal	$114,000
Total Assets	$3,115,000

Liabilities

All amounts owed to others should be stated in the liabilities section of the personal financial statement. In many cases, the items listed will be owed on the assets already stated in the assets section of the financial statement.

Sample Personal Financial Statement: Liabilities Listing

Credit Cards: This is a listing of the balances outstanding on all credit cards for which you are responsible.	
Visa (Third Pacific Bank)	$4,000
Mastercard (Second Atlantic Bank)	2,000
Subtotal	$6,000
Unsecured Loans: This is any obligations payable to other parties that are unsecured by any assets; that is, you have pledged no collateral on these loans.	
Rapper Bank (balloon term loan, interest payable quarterly at 9%, due 12/1/X3)	$15,000
Subtotal	$15,000
Secured Loans: This is any obligations payable to other parties that are secured by assets; this may be real estate or personal assets.	
Bank of the Midwest (mortgage on personal residence, 5%, due 6/30/X1)	$500,000
Steamboat Trust (mortgage on vacation home, 6%, due 3/15/X2)	750,000
Subtotal	$1,250,000
Other Liabilities: This is any remaining obligations not already stated, such as tax bills and unpaid alimony.	
Income tax bill to state of Colorado	$4,000
Unpaid alimony	6,000
Subtotal	$10,000
Total Liabilities	$1,281,000
Net Worth	$1,834,000

The net worth figure at the bottom of the preceding exhibit is your total assets minus your total liabilities. If the net worth figure is negative (where your liabilities exceed your assets), it will be exceedingly difficult to borrow money; lenders will shy away from anyone who is in a financially tenuous position.

Income and Expenses

The final part of your personal financial statement is a listing of all annual income and expenses. We separate these items into two statements, as noted in the following two exhibits.

Sample Personal Financial Statement: Annual Income

Salary and Wages: This is a listing of all wages paid to you, as well as earnings from being an independent contractor, and the earnings from operating your own business.	
Double Tree Groceries (primary employer)	$110,000
Acme Household Assistance (independent contractor work)	10,000
Subtotal	$120,000
Income from Receivables: This is a statement of the cash received from any receivables that other parties owe to you, including loans. State the entire amount of these receipts, not just the interest portion.	
Albert Ellingwood ($80/month)	$960
Carl Blaurock ($60/month)	720
Subtotal	$1,680
Income from Rental Property: This is a listing of the cash received from renting out property. If there are plans to alter the rent, state the timing and amount of the change.	
Steamboat vacation home, rental of	$8,000
Subtotal	$8,000
Income from Dividends and Interest: This is the amount of cash received from dividends and interest, stated by source. These sources should match the asset sources listed in the assets portion of the personal financial statement.	
Amalgamated Concrete dividends	$3,000
Savings account interest (Second Atlantic Bank)	320
Subtotal	$3,320
Other Income: This is all remaining sources of income, such as ongoing payments for disability, trust fund payments, and alimony payments.	
Disability payments (U.S. military)	$250
Trust fund payments	1,750
Subtotal	$2,000
Total Annual Income	**$135,000**

The intent behind the compilation of an expenses listing is to determine how much it costs you to live. This can be the most difficult of the various statements to compile, because expenses routinely include any number of outlier expenses that are not recurring, such as medical bills related to a car accident, or roof repairs related to hail damage. The decision to include or exclude these outlier expenses is essentially driven by the extent to which they might happen again. A truly extraordinary, once-in-a-lifetime expense can be excluded, while an expense that is not frequent but which will recur should probably be included. A sample expenses statement appears in the following exhibit.

Sample Personal Financial Statement: Expenses

Rent/Mortgage Loan Payments: This is the annual payments made for rent or the mortgage on a residence.	
Bank of the Midwest (on primary residence)	$25,000
Steamboat Trust (on vacation residence)	20,000
Subtotal	$45,000
Property Taxes: This is all taxes paid on your property holdings.	
County property taxes on primary residence	$2,000
County property taxes on vacation residence	2,000
Subtotal	$4,000
Other Loan Payments: This is the payments made on all loans not associated with real estate, such as student loan payments.	
Rapper Bank (balloon term loan)	$1,350
Subtotal	$1,350
Living Expenses: This is all expenses associated with your ongoing living expenses that are not included elsewhere in this statement, such as insurance, utilities, food, clothing, travel, and medical care.	
Food expenses	$7,000
Clothing expenses	3,000
Medical expenses	12,000
Utility expenses	4,000
Insurance expenses	2,000
Other living expenses	9,000
Subtotal	$37,000

Income Taxes: This is both federal and state income taxes paid. If the rates have changed recently, then include the estimated tax that will be paid in the current year.	
Annual federal income tax payment	$24,000
Annual state income tax payment	2,650
Subtotal	$26,650
Other Income: This is all remaining expenses, typically expenditures made on a one-time basis, such as the replacement of a major appliance, holiday vacations, and child support payments.	
Child support payments	$12,000
Subtotal	$12,000
Total Expenses	**$126,000**

When combined, the personal income and expense exhibits show that this individual is generating $9,000 of net income per year. In the example, finding that there is only $9,000 of excess cash per year might lead you to the reasonable conclusion that it does not make sense to apply for a mortgage that will require a larger annual repayment amount than $9,000.

Summary

By far the largest cash outflow issue that any real estate investor faces is paying for mortgages. This means that you need to spend a great deal of time weighing the features of various mortgage products, to find the one that matches your specific cash flow requirements. This may involve a tradeoff between points and the interest rate charged, reducing fees in favor of a higher interest rate, or perhaps accepting a variable-rate mortgage in order to minimize short-term cash flows. There is no ideal mortgage product for everyone; you will need to make that decision based on your personal circumstances, as well as the cash flows expected from the property you want to acquire.

Chapter 3
Evaluating Properties

Introduction

In this chapter, we describe the types of research you should conduct in order to find just the right property. This includes regional analysis, local market analysis, and barriers to entry. When scouting the market for available real estate, keep in mind the key goal – which is to acquire property in the right location *and* at the right price. The focus tends to be on location, but a great location is worthless if the price is not reasonable.

Where to Invest

When deciding upon your ideal location within which to conduct searches for real estate, it is best to initially confine yourself to the immediate area – such as within a one-hour drive. Doing so concentrates your attention on a limited area, so that you can engage in a "deep dive" and really learn all facets of a region, rather than watering down your attention over a broad swathe of territory. In addition, limiting your driving range to a property makes it easier to personally deal with any problems that may arise, should you choose to purchase a property.

It is entirely possible that your local area is not a good real estate market at the moment. Perhaps a shaky local economy has put employment into a tailspin, so that potential renters are evacuating the area in search of employment elsewhere. If so, expand your investing area to a more distant, specifically-defined area – but incorporate into this selection the extra amount of travel time. It can be quite difficult to monitor the conditions in a distant region, especially when you have responsibilities in your current location, such as family commitments or a full-time job.

No matter where you choose to focus your investing activities, be sure to have local contacts who can assist with the many issues associated with real estate investing, including a property manager, real estate agent, lender, and attorney. Without these connections, it can be nearly impossible to conduct efficient investment activities. Also, without on-site assistants to monitor properties, it is far more likely that bad tenants will trash them, or that empty properties suffer from vandalism. In short, do not try to invest in distant areas on a solo basis.

Regional Analysis

Part of the selection process for a particular region is to research the economic viability of the surrounding area. If a number of large employers have left the area, then rental demand will likely be weak, and it is best not to invest in the area. Other indicators of economic viability are trends in the population level over the past few years, as well as the rate of job growth. It is also worthwhile to research the average rental rate and occupancy rate (for commercial or residential real estate, depending on your preference). Real estate appraisers can also provide this information. The local bank may employ an analyst, who tracks this information. Banks require it in order to detect trends that could adversely impact their loan loss rates.

> **Tip:** If lenders are unhappy about providing a loan and your credit rating is good, the remaining variable is that their analysis department is unhappy about the economic fundamentals for the area in which you propose to acquire property.

A good source of information for a regional analysis is the *metropolitan statistical area*, which is a geographical region with a relatively high population density at its core and close economic ties throughout the area. The Census Bureau collects information at this level of detail, which is then analyzed and disseminated by the Bureau of Labor Statistics.

When reviewing the Census Bureau's data, pay particular attention to changes in population growth. The demand for real estate is primarily based on the population level in the local area. Whenever the population increases, there is more demand for residential housing, service providers, and office space. Conversely, stagnant or declining populations result in weak real estate demand, and therefore less of an opportunity to make profitable investments in real estate. Real estate developers pay particular attention to population growth rates by individual neighborhood, since this information is the key driver of demand for rental units in those areas.

Another strong indicator of real estate demand is job growth. Whenever a new employer moves into an area, the jobs it creates trigger an immediate demand for housing, usually in the range of 1-2 new jobs generating demand for one additional household. In addition, these new jobs create more demand for commercial office space of many types, including hairdressers, grocery stores, gyms, and so forth.

> **Tip:** The demand for real estate will be much higher when the jobs being created in the local area are high-paying. The people employed in these positions will have much more disposable income with which to pay for housing, which is not the case when new jobs are of the low-paying variety.

It is useful to keep track of all development actions taken by the local government. For example, a government may elect to install new roads, build airports and subways, and so forth. These investments tend to foster economic growth, and so are strong indicators of job creation, which in turn creates demand for real estate.

A further area of analysis is the extent to which a target area is diversified. For example, if a single manufacturing plant provides employment for the majority of the adults in a target area, then this is a risk for the investor – if that facility closes its doors, the local real estate market will be destroyed for years, unless new employers can be convinced to move to the area. Conversely, if employment is spread across a number of employers and industries, then it is a good bet that no single employer failure will have much of an impact on the surrounding area.

A variation on the concept of job diversification is investigating whether the jobs in the area are of the high-growth or low-growth variety. For example, if a city houses the state government, its job growth is likely to be slower, since there is little growth in government jobs. Conversely, if the main employers are high technology firms that are growing rapidly, then it is a good bet that the number of jobs will increase at a brisk pace in the near future. That being said, areas that employ large numbers of government or health care workers tend to have more consistent long-term demand for real estate, since these jobs are the least likely to be lost during an economic downturn.

Besides economic activity, it is also useful to investigate whether the properties in your selected region are already overpriced. This is especially common in what are considered to be the "best" neighborhoods, where buyers have repeatedly bid up property prices to the point where there is no room for any additional price appreciation. It is useful to spot these areas, so that you can block them out and turn your attention to more underpriced neighborhoods.

Overall, it is more important to invest in a region that is experiencing buoyant economic and population growth, since the overall level of demand will be high in these areas, even if the exact property location is not the best. Conversely, your returns may be quite poor in an area where a property is perfectly positioned, but the local economy is in a tailspin.

Local Market Analysis

In the following sub-sections, we cover several ways in which to analyze a local market at a granular level.

Indicators of Supply and Demand

Thus far, we have only discussed the impact of regional issues on the real estate market. At a more granular level, the key factor is supply and demand. If there is a great deal of demand for real estate and only a limited supply, then property prices will inevitably appreciate. In the reverse situation, prices will decline. A high-demand market is called a seller's market, where sellers are receiving multiple offers above their asking price. In a buyer's market, sellers are being forced to lower their asking price and offer seller financing in order to get rid of their property.

There are a number of indicators of supply and demand, which are as follows:

- *Building permits*. The number of building permits issued is a supply indicator. This is the earliest indicator of an increase in supply, which may not result in property actually being available for a year or more. When there is a sustained trend of building permits being granted, there is a good chance that the supply of real estate will eventually exceed demand. This information is available from the local government's planning department.
- *Rate of new property absorption*. This is the rate at which new buildings are rented and occupied, and is considered a supply indicator. It is measured in the number of housing units for residential property, and in square footage for commercial property. A good sign of a market worth investing in is where

new property is promptly rented, perhaps within a few months. It is best to watch absorption on a trend line, to get a feel for whether the rate of absorption is increasing or decreasing over time. This information is available from real estate brokers.

- *Duration of property listings.* The duration of property listings is a supply indicator. When properties have been on the market for an extended time, it can indicate either excessive supply or weak demand, though it also could be related to an excessively high asking price or problems with a specific property.
- *Occupancy rate.* This is the percentage of a property type that is currently being rented. For example, if there are 3,000 residential rental units currently being rented in a designated market and the occupancy rate is 98%, then that means 60 of the units are currently vacant. This calculation is expressed in square feet for commercial properties. This is an indicator of demand, where a high occupancy rate usually leads to price appreciation in the near term, with the reverse occurring when the occupancy rate is low. It can be quite difficult to collect occupancy data, especially since so many units are rented out directly by owners, who do not share this information with anyone. Local trade organizations may conduct periodic surveys to collect this information.
- *Rental rates.* Local rental rates are a demand indicator, and are especially useful when tracked on a trend line. A concern here is that some owners report a rather high rental rate but then offer concessions from it, such as an initial month of free rent, so the actual rental rate net of these effects can be difficult to discern.

EXAMPLE

Larry is investigating the rental rates being offered within a limited region. He contacts the property manager for a 50-unit apartment complex, and learns that units are renting for $1,800 per month. However, lessees are also given two months of free rent, which means that the effective monthly rate is only $1,500. This arrangement exists because the local real estate market is rather weak, and the owner of the complex does not want any older tenants to complain that newer tenants are getting a better deal.

The preceding indicators usually work in concert to reveal a consistent outcome; they rarely present conflicting messages. Thus, if there are few building permits being issued, occupancy levels are low, and rental rates are declining, it is a good bet that demand is quite weak, and you should be investing elsewhere. The ideal situation is the reverse, where demand greatly exceeds supply. When this condition exists, property owners can increase rents, avoid rent concessions, and minimize tenant improvement allowances – resulting in strong positive cash flows.

Other Local Market Issues

The single most significant negative factor in a local market is the crime rate. An area with a high crime rate is likely to have both a great deal of supply (since everyone wants to leave) and very little demand (since no one wants to buy there). In addition, there is an increased risk that the property will be vandalized. The local sheriff's office can provide information about recent crimes in the area that you are researching. Another issue that can be of concern if you are renting residential property is the location of any registered sex offenders. This information is usually available from the state database for sex offenders (though the quality of these databases varies by state).

Other considerations arise when you are planning to invest in commercial real estate for professionals. If so, check the area for access to public transit, such as bus routes and subways. Also, see if there is adequate retail space in the area to support anyone working in your proposed building, such as restaurants and grocery shopping. Professionals are especially picky about their selections of office space, so be sure to only invest in areas where the proper mix of these features is available.

Yet another issue worth investigating is tax assessments. Some areas are subject to special property tax assessments, perhaps related to the construction of schools, a sports stadium, or light rail. While these assessments may be worthwhile, you should know the exact boundaries of these assessment districts, in case it is possible to acquire property just outside of them.

A significant driver of property values is the quality of adjacent schools. Parents with children are willing to pay substantially more to send their children to a high-quality school, so pay attention to the ratings for the schools within your target area. In addition, the people who want high-quality schools and who own businesses will be inclined to work in locations near their homes, so school quality also has a positive impact on commercial property prices. This is an even more significant issue when there is a high-quality university nearby. Employers are more likely to set up shop near these institutions, since doing so gives them a better chance to hire graduates.

A final issue to consider is how well homes are maintained within the area. A high level of quality care across multiple properties, even if they are relatively inexpensive properties, can have a significant positive impact on local home prices. Even better, a high level of care could be the result of an aggressive homeowners' association that enforces strict compliance with the association's maintenance requirements. You can only discern these conditions by driving through the area; this is a tough issue to identify if you live hours away.

> **Tip:** The preceding paragraph contained a critical point; you cannot improve the value of your property when the surrounding properties look slovenly. Increases in property values is a group effort.

Investing Near Infrastructure

One of the best ways to profit from substantial property appreciation is to acquire property near new infrastructure projects. For example, the construction of a shopping mall or an airport will inevitably lead to demand from the people who will eventually work there, with ancillary demand coming from the businesses supporting those households. The increased demand for real estate will allow for above-average rental rates, higher occupancy levels, and higher property valuations.

Tip: The major retail chains conduct extensive investigations of the local area before they build a store, so a safe bet is to acquire property near one of their stores.

The same approach can be applied to redevelopment districts. A local government offers funding and/or tax incentives to any real estate developers that want to redevelop a blighted area. Investing in these areas early can result in a substantial boost in your return on investment, since property values can appreciate particularly quickly in these areas. However, be warned that some of these projects are not completed, so deciding when to invest in these areas can be a critical decision – do you invest early and run the risk that the project will not be finished, or wait and then buy property at a much higher price?

Barriers to Entry

When evaluating a local area for investment opportunities, be aware of any barriers to entry. For example, NIMBY residents (not in my back yard) are adamantly opposed to additional construction in their neighborhoods, especially high-rise apartment buildings that they consider to be unsightly, or anything else that will increase the amount of congestion near them. NIMBY opposition will make it extremely difficult to construct new property, but it also constrains supply within the area – resulting in increased property prices. Consequently, if you can acquire property in a NIMBY area and are willing to own it for an extended period of time, a likely outcome is above-average appreciation in the market price of the property.

Another barrier to entry naturally arises when all available land has been built out. This is especially common in areas that are restricted from expansion by a lake, mountain range, or park. In this situation, the only way for anyone to add capacity is to scrape an existing property and build a new one that contains more square footage. Again, the lack of supply should result in property appreciation, but be aware that this restriction may cause potential tenants to look elsewhere for affordable space.

Yet another barrier to entry is environmental concerns in the area, such as the required remediation of a toxic waste dump before any structures can be built. These requirements are exceptionally costly, typically making it unprofitable to build any property. A variation on the concept is the government designation of certain land as wetland, which means that no construction will be allowed on the land at all. Yet another variation is when the government requires the completion of an expensive environmental impact statement before construction will be authorized. The net effect of these issues in some areas can be severe, effectively curtailing any new construction.

The Real Estate Cycle

Any market is likely to go through an ongoing series of fluctuations, sometimes resulting in a buyer's market and sometimes in a seller's market. High levels of demand may lead to too much new construction, resulting in a decline in property prices and no incentive for builders to construct new properties. After a period of time when few new properties are being added to the market, demand catches up with and exceeds supply, resulting in a seller's market once again, along with the attendant construction boom.

The real estate cycle presents an opportunity for timing the market. This is somewhat different from the buy-low, sell-high mantra associated with the stock market, where the assumption is that investors are regularly churning their shareholdings. In real estate, the mantra is more like buy-low and keep it, since many investors are willing to retain their properties for decades. This means piling up your cash during peak periods in the real estate cycle, waiting perhaps for several years until prices return to more normal levels, and then acquiring property. However, if it appears that property even in a hot market is likely to keep appreciating, you may want to take a risk and purchase a property at a relatively high price.

The Core Elements of an Investment

The goal of real estate investing is to create a return on investment that is greater than your cost of funds. This can be achieved by either increasing the revenues generated by a property or by reducing its expenses. This brings up the question of why the current owner does not do so – it is likely that someone is telling a tall tale if they insist that the current list price of a property is justified simply by jacking up the rent once you take ownership. Instead, you will need to search for indicators of circumstances that can realistically result in either a rent increase or an expense decline. Consider the following possibilities:

- *High demand.* A property is already fully rented, and the property manager has a list of people waiting to rent as soon as space becomes available. In this case, the property really is in high demand, so a judicious rent increase might be a possibility.
- *Low turnover.* A property is already fully rented, and there is very little turnover among the tenants. The absence of turnover is a strong indicator that rents can be increased, since the current tenants are clearly not finding better options elsewhere.
- *Older owner.* Some property owners who are nearing retirement find the sale process uncomfortable, and so deliberately set their asking price low in order to close a deal as quickly as possible and with minimal fuss.
- *Quick sale.* The owner of a property wants to sell as soon as possible, and is willing to accept a below-market price in order to do so. This is most likely when the current owner has an immediate need for cash, as can be the case with a divorce or the declining health of someone in the owner's family.

- *Uniform rents*. The owner of a property has set the same rental rates for every unit. This presents a targeted opportunity for rental increases, where the rent on more desirable unit locations can be increased. For example, the rent on rooms facing away from a busy road can justifiably be increased, on the grounds that traffic noise is reduced.

It may be possible to add value to an investment property by acquiring better tenants. This means finding tenants with solid financial statements, and especially ones that are willing to enter into long-term leases. If it is possible to acquire tenants of this type, the total cash inflow from a property will rise (even without a rent increase), because the property is more consistently filled with paying tenants; there are no cash flow declines due to rental space being unoccupied.

Rent Control

Rent control is a government-imposed requirement that caps the amount of rent that can be charged on a property. It is most commonly applied in dense urban environments where demand greatly exceeds supply, so that rental rates are extremely high. Imposing a rental cap allows lower-income people to afford living in the area. Because rent control reduces the amount of cash inflow from a property, the normal rate of property appreciation cannot be achieved. In addition, property expenses will likely increase over time as a property ages, but the cost cannot be passed through to tenants without the prior approval of a rent control board. In short, it is an exceptionally bad idea to invest in rent controlled real estate, unless you are willing to take a chance that the controls will be removed in the near future.

The Summary Page

Now that we have identified a number of key items to investigate for the region in which you want to invest, it makes sense to formalize the investigation with a summary page. This information will be requested by anyone who wants to lease space from you. For example, how far is it to the nearest bus stop, grocery store, gym, hospital, restaurant, dry cleaner's, police station, pharmacy, post office, and day care facility? Having this information available answers all key questions that a tenant might ask, and allows for a quicker decision.

If you are considering several properties within the region, prepare this summary page for each one, adding on the square footage, parking, and other amenities associated with each one. Doing so makes it much easier to compare the properties and decide which one represents the best investment.

Summary

The discussion in this chapter identified a number of issues that you should investigate as part of the evaluation process that leads up to the purchase of a property. Keep in mind that this investigation does not end with the purchase of a property. You should continue to monitor these issues, to see if the quality of the area is trending up or down. If the trend is upward, you might want to consider investing in another property. If the trend is dropping, consider selling out and shifting your funds elsewhere.

Chapter 4
Property Income Issues

Introduction

Thus far, we have mostly addressed the myriads of issues associated with finding the right property, which is the cash outflow side of real estate investing. Of equal importance is the cash inflows earned from leasing out the property. In this chapter, we discuss the nature of a lease and its value.

The Nature of a Lease

A *lease* is an arrangement under which a lessor agrees to allow a lessee to use specified real property for a stated period of time in exchange for a series of payments.

> **Tip:** Always prepare a written lease that is signed by both parties. Otherwise, it will be quite difficult to enforce a verbal arrangement when a lessee refuses to make a payment or conform to other aspects of the lease.

There are three types of leases in use. In a *gross lease* arrangement, the lessor pays for nearly all of the operating expenses associated with a property. This approach increases the risk for the lessor, who will have to absorb any unusually high operating expenses incurred by the tenants. This risk can be mitigated by using a *modified gross lease* instead, where the lessees are responsible for some of the expenses incurred. For example, a tenant may be responsible for paying its own electricity bill, or to pay for its janitorial costs. A more advanced form of the modified gross lease is the *net lease*, where lessees are responsible for most of the operating costs incurred, such as property taxes, maintenance, insurance, and utilities. When lessees are responsible for the payment of essentially all costs, the underlying lease is called a *triple net lease*.

> **Tip:** A residential property lease is usually set up as a gross lease, though the tenant may pay for utilities. This is because the owner wants to be responsible for all maintenance, to ensure that the property is in a good state of repair.

> **Tip:** Multi-unit properties should always have separate metering for electricity, gas, and water, so that the related billings can be charged straight through to tenants.

The Value of a Lease

When you purchase property, one or more parties may already be leasing space within it. If so, you should examine these leases as part of your due diligence on the property, since they show several possible risks and opportunities. When reviewing these documents, consider the following items:

- *Will any leases be voided?* The vast majority of all leases are linked to the property, and so will continue in force even when ownership of the property changes. However, some leases contain a clause that allows the lessee to void the agreement in the event of an ownership change. You should certainly be aware of the existence of these clauses, especially when they are included in the lease of a major tenant.
- *Are any leases about to expire?* When a lease is about to expire, it always raises some uncertainty about whether a tenant will renew. If it appears that a tenant will leave, you need to consider the cost to persuade this party to stay, such as a period of free rent or tenant improvements.

Tip: It is nearly always worthwhile to persuade an existing tenant to renew a lease, rather than searching for a replacement tenant. This is because the costs to advertise the property, as well as to clean and update it for a new tenant, can be substantial. And don't forget that the unit may stand empty for many months, until a new tenant can be found.

- *Can any leases be renewed?* Many leases contain a renewal option, which allows a lessee to extend the terms of a lease – usually with an inflationary boost in the rental rate. Any of these arrangements involving below-market rates will certainly be of interest, since you will be unable to raise the rent beyond the terms specified in the renewal option.
- *Have any concessions not been fulfilled?* An existing rent agreement might contain concessions that have not yet been fulfilled. For example, an office lease might state that new carpeting will be installed during January of the following year, or that rent will be free in December. Be aware of these obligations, and factor them into your cash flow projections.
- *Are extra fees specified?* In order to charge tenants for a variety of fees, such as returned checks and late payments, the associated terms must be stated in the lease document. If they are not mentioned, then you have no enforceable way to collect these charges.
- *Can any rents be increased?* Some leases may have been set at below-market rates, while there may be no rent escalation clause in other leases. A useful analysis is whether a tenant is likely to stay if you increase their rent at the next lease renewal, or whether you can readily find a replacement if they depart. When a tenant occupies highly customized space (such as a brew pub), it is much less likely to depart the premises, even in the face of quite a substantial rent increase.

Tip: As part of the due diligence process, always demand a complete copy of each lease, and forward them to your attorney for review. This is your last chance to spot leasing issues before you acquire a property.

When there are flaws in the lease agreements, this does not represent an automatic failing grade for a property. However, they *can* reduce the value of the property, because it will not be possible to maximize revenues until the lease agreements expire and are replaced with more favorable ones.

> **Tip:** If you elect to purchase a property, try to standardize all tenants on the same lease agreement. Doing so makes it easier to monitor what tenants are allowed to do, and which fees apply to them.

The preceding analysis of leases is much easier for residential properties than for commercial ones. Commercial tenants have far more exacting requirements; this calls for the preparation of a summary document for each lease, called a *lease abstract*, which contains such information as a tenant's name, square footage, renewal options, tenant improvements, security deposits, additional fees, and whether a party has the first right of refusal for leasing additional space. Creating lease abstracts provides investors with the following benefits:

- *Risk mitigation.* Understanding the terms of all lease agreements reduces the risk of making a costly mistake. It is especially useful for avoiding missing crucial dates, such as when a rent increase is scheduled to go into effect, or when taxes can be charged through to tenants.
- *Revenue generation.* It is easier to peruse a lease abstract to spot rent provisions that the prior owner might have missed, which can be billed through to the tenant. This is an especially likely opportunity when the current property manager does not monitor when rent increases are supposed to occur, as per the underlying lease agreements.
- *Comparisons.* When you are comparing several properties for potential purchase, it is useful to compare the lease abstracts associated with these properties. Differences in the leases can be the deciding factor for selecting a property.

> **Tip:** An excellent place to look for revenue generation is in the terms of any percentage rent arrangements, where a retailer is required to pay the landlord a base rent plus a percentage of its sales. These can be complex arrangements, so be sure to review them in detail to see if any rent was not paid.

> **Tip:** If you have commercial tenants, ask them for annual financial statements. This is a good way to determine whether they are in declining financial health, in which case you can start planning for replacement tenants.

The Rent Roll

Any party selling a rental property should be able to provide a *rent roll*, which is a list of the rent earned from each unit. This is the essential property income report, since it shows all cash inflows in a summarized format. A sample rent roll appears in the following exhibit.

Sample Rent Roll

Unit	Tenant	Prior Balance	Current Rent	Receipt Date	Other Payments	Description	Receipt Total	Balance Due
A	Abrams	$1,000	$1,000	12/1	$--	--	$2,000	$--
B	Bester	--	2,000	12/2	100	Parking	2,100	--
C	Chelsey	500	1,800	12/1	75	Parking	2,375	--
D	Diddle	--	2,200	12/1	250	Storage	2,200	250
E	Enderby	--	1,900	12/3	--	--	1,900	--
F	Fallow	1,000	1,500	12/2	100	Late fee	2,600	--
		$2,500	$10,400		$525		$13,175	$250

Summary

The primary revenue source from an investment property is the ongoing rent payments received from tenants. These payments are based on the underlying lease agreements, so it makes sense to have a detailed understanding of the terms of these leases prior to making an offer to purchase a property. Once a property has been purchased, you should compile a lease abstract for each lease, making it easier to monitor the essentials of each one.

Chapter 5
Property Valuation

Introduction

What factors drive the valuation of a property? It is useful to understand several different approaches to valuation, so that you can develop a range of possible valuations. In this chapter, we describe a number of valuation methods, including the broker price opinion, sales comparisons, replacement cost, and income capitalization – along with several supporting concepts.

The Drivers of Value

We have indicated earlier in this book that the main drivers of property value are supply and demand. That is a very high-level view of the situation. A deeper look at the situation reveals that there are other drivers of value. Yes, demand is a key driver, but it is demand by those with the financial means to make a purchase. Having financial means is not driven just by the amount of a buyer's available cash, but also by the lending environment. If interest rates are high, then fewer investors will be willing to purchase property. And in highly restrictive credit environments, lenders may not be willing to lend money to anyone except those with the most perfect credit histories. Conversely, when rates are low and the system is awash in cash, nearly anyone can gain access to a mortgage, which greatly increases demand.

Another driver of value is the utility of the property in question. A property that thoroughly meets a need will receive the highest valuation. For example, a property located in an area that experiences a high level of foot traffic is perfect for a retail store. Conversely, a property located at the end of a side street is not suitable for a retail store, and so would command a much lower price. Similarly, an apartment complex immediately adjacent to public transportation and a grocery store would be considered highly suitable by tenants, while parents would consider a housing development situated next to a highly-rated school to be an ideal location. One of the best ways to generate a run-up in property value is to acquire a run-down property in a high-utility location and fix it up; doing so will make it much easier to charge the presumably high rent levels being levied elsewhere in the area.

The inverse of having high utility is when a property is located in a run-down area. When the general maintenance level is low, there are abandoned properties, and crime rates are high, this has a strong negative impact on the value of your property – no matter how well maintained it may be.

A factor that can greatly impact property values (up or down) is the scarcity of a property. For example, a log cabin situated in a forest is not scarce if there are thousands of other cabins located in the same forest. Conversely, if it is the only cabin in the area because the government does not allow construction anywhere else in the forest, then the cabin can certainly be considered scarce, and so will command a high price. The same concept applies to beachfront properties – there is only so much available land alongside a waterway, so those lucky enough to own property there will experience higher valuation increases than elsewhere.

Another driver of value is the concept of substitution, which holds that a buyer will not pay more for a property than the price being offered for a similar property. For example, the prices of all condominiums in a condo tower are inextricably linked together, since they all have similar floor plans and views. Anyone buying or selling one of these units will be able to do so within a narrow range established by the prices at which similar units have sold.

The concept of conformity can certainly impact a property's value. Generally, a property that looks similar to and fits in with the surrounding properties will command a higher valuation than one that does not. This can present an opportunity, where you could acquire a non-conforming property and make those changes needed to bring it into alignment with the surrounding properties. The conformity concept also means that it is not cost-effective to over-improve a property, since it will then be an outlier in the neighborhood.

A final driver of value is the ease with which property rights can be transferred from a seller to a buyer. This is primarily a concern when investing in other countries, where governments limit property ownership to their own citizens.

The Highest and Best Use Concept

When reviewing investment properties, a key consideration is whether it is currently being applied in the best possible way. As an investor, you will want to generate the highest possible return, which may mean altering the function of a property to one that earns a greater return. For example, a homeowner in a prime location in a large city has stubbornly refused to sell out to developers for years. If you were to acquire the property following the homeowner's death, would you really rent it out as a single-family home, or would it make more sense to resell the property to a developer who will replace it with a high-rise apartment complex?

The highest and best use concept can vary over time, as neighborhoods change and governments alter the zoning laws. For example, a neighborhood has gradually declined over the years, and now the planning commission has altered its zoning to also allow for light industrial facilities. In this situation, it can make sense to sell out to a warehouse development company, since that is now the highest and best use of the property.

> **Note:** You may get into a bidding war with another investor and be massively outbid by the other party. This is likely because the other investor has reviewed the property information and concluded that it can be put to an alternative use that will yield higher returns – thereby justifying the higher bid price.

How to Derive a Property Value

The typical starting point for the derivation of a property's value is to call your real estate agent and request a broker price opinion (BPO). A BPO is based on the characteristics of the property being considered. It is not representative of an official appraised value, nor will it necessarily correspond to the property's market value. Some of the factors that a broker will consider when developing a price opinion include the value of similar surrounding properties and sales trends in the neighborhood. The location of the property and its place among its surroundings factor into the opinion. Comparable listings and recent sales also affect the BPO. Agents also take into account an estimate of the costs associated with getting the property ready for sale, as well as the cost of any needed repairs. Given the many variables associated with real estate, a group of agents might all come up with somewhat different price estimates.

Rather than relying entirely on a BPO, you should calculate several additional measurements. One possibility is the *gross rent multiplier*. To calculate it, divide the proposed purchase price by the annual rent associated with a property. For example, if the price of a property is $600,000 and the annual rent associated with it is $40,000, then its gross rent multiplier is 15. This measure can be useful for comparing several properties that you are considering purchasing, to determine which one generates the best return in relation to its purchase price.

Tip: It is possible that the current property owner raised the rent rates just prior to putting the property on the market, thereby maximizing the gross rent multiplier, so that the property carries an artificially high value. Another concern with this practice is that you will not realistically be able to raise the rent again for some time, until rental rates in the area rise enough to warrant an increase.

A concern with the gross rent multiplier is that it does not account for the operating expenses associated with a property – only its gross income. This can be highly misleading, since the multiplier might indicate that a property generates a reasonable return, while the reality is that its operating expenses (especially when the property is an older one and in need of repair) result in deep losses. A further concern is that the multiplier is based solely on the current gross rent generated, without any indication of whether any of the underlying leases will soon expire. It is entirely possible that the seller has timed the sale to coincide with full occupancy, knowing that rents are likely to decline in the near future. This is a particular concern when rents are near their seasonal peak, after which they go into a steep decline during the offseason.

EXAMPLE

Anna is evaluating whether she should purchase either of two apartment properties. One is a relatively old property that only allows tenants who are at least 55 years old. People in this age group rarely party, and so cause minimal damage. In addition, more than half the residents have been there for over a decade. The second property is about the same age, but specializes in short-term tenants who work at the local chicken processing plant; the current owner has only invested in the most minimal maintenance activities. Both properties can be acquired for $1 million. The senior living complex is clearly the better property, since its rents are more stable and it requires much less maintenance.

Another measurement possibility is the *price per square foot*. It is calculated by dividing a property's asking price by the number of square feet of the building. For example, if the price of a property is $600,000 and it contains 6,000 square feet, then its price per square foot is $100. While this measurement is useful for comparing properties, it is too simplistic to drive an investment decision. It does not address a variety of other issues, such as the location of the property, how well it was constructed, the current occupancy rate, or what types of amenities it contains. That being said, it can serve to quickly identify outlier properties that are clearly priced too high for the surrounding area, and which can therefore be ignored. Similarly, it might draw your attention to an unusually low-cost property for further investigation.

A final measurement possibility is *replacement cost*. This is the cost that you would incur in order to build a comparable property in the same location, and which fulfills the same function. This can be an involved and expensive process, which may not be a cost-effective approach when trying to gain a quick understanding of a property's value. The simplest approach is to find a standard construction cost per square foot for a similar structure in the same market, and multiply it by the square footage of the property under investigation. This analysis should include the cost of the land on which the property is situated. Any properties that can be acquired for less than their replacement cost are worth investigating further.

While the calculations noted here are relatively easy to derive, they do not provide sufficient information to make an informed decision about how much to pay for a property. In order to do so, we continue with several other valuation concepts in the following sections.

The Return on Property Investment

When deciding whether the price of a property represents an acceptable investment, you should understand the concept of *return on investment* (ROI). At a high level, it refers to the annual return generated from a property, divided into its purchase price. For example, a property that costs $1,000,000 and returns $80,000 per year generates an ROI of 8%.

While the basic calculation is easy enough, there are a number of underlying factors that can make it difficult to achieve the ROI that you might have calculated when you first contemplated the purchase of a property. The key factors are aggregated as follows into items impacting the numerator (the return) and the denominator (the investment):

Numerator Issues

- *Tenant turnover.* When tenants do not renew their leases, there is likely to be some downtime while new tenants are found. It may also be necessary to advertise these openings, as well as to pay a commission to a leasing agency and renovate the empty space for the new tenant.
- *Defaults.* Some tenants may be in difficult financial circumstances, and so cannot pay the rent when it is due (or ever). Besides the obvious resulting decline in revenue, this may also trigger legal expenses to pursue the tenants for payment or to evict them. The property restoration costs to recover from an evicted tenant tend to be particularly high.
- *Unexpected expenses.* It may be necessary to make substantial expenditures to maintain a property, especially when a property is an older one where the original construction quality was below average.
- *Rent management.* Your ability to increase rents will depend to some extent on the rent rates being offered on comparable properties in the immediate area; these local rates are not under your control, so this can be an area of considerable uncertainty.
- *Interest rate variations.* If the property was purchased with a variable-rate loan, then changes in the interest rate over time will impact the amount of expense incurred to service the loan.

Denominator Issues

- *Overpayment.* Becoming overly attached to a property or buying it through a bidding war can result in overpaying for it. If so, it will be extremely difficult to ever generate a reasonable return on investment, given that the denominator of the ROI calculation is simply too large.

An additional factor that can be incorporated into the ROI concept is the appreciation in value of a property over time. In hot property markets, appreciation can result in a greater return than any of the ongoing cash flows derived from a property.

Net Operating Income

Net operating income is a measure of the profitability of a real estate investment. It is used to examine the underlying cash flows of an investment before the effects of taxes and financing costs are considered. A high net operating income figure should result in a higher property valuation.

The calculation of net operating income is to subtract all operating expenses from the revenues generated by a property. The formula is:

+	Revenue generated by real estate
-	Operating expenses
=	Net operating income

The revenues associated with a property may include much more than lease income. Other revenues for residential properties may include parking fees, late fees, returned check charges, laundry proceeds, service charges, Internet fees, storage charges, and vending proceeds. Several additional charges may apply to commercial properties, such as supplemental heating and air conditioning during off-work hours, common area maintenance charges, and security fees.

The operating expenses associated with a property include janitorial expenses, property insurance, property management fees, property taxes, repairs and maintenance, and utilities. Expenses not included in the operating expenses category include interest expense and income taxes. Capital expenditures are also not included in the formulation of operating expenses.

Tip: The current owner of a property may understate the operating expenses of a property by cutting back on expenditures in the prior year, thereby making the property appear to be more valuable than is really the case.

When deciding whether to buy a property, a detailed analysis of its net operating income is *always* warranted – not just on a current basis, but also on a projected basis, in case you suspect that some of these revenue or expense items will change in the future. Ideally, a future projection should extend several years into the future. While the current net operating income can be derived from information provided by the current property owner (subject to the issue noted in the following tip), deriving projections is quite a bit more difficult; you should consider the following items:

- Which tenants will renew their leases? If so, at what rate, and what concessions will need to be offered? This calls for a detailed analysis of every lease agreement, noting the projected lease payments associated with each one. Do not rely on a summary provided by the current owner; develop your own analysis.
- Will any tenants be unable to make their lease payments on time? This will call for a review of their payment histories to detect payment patterns. If their financial statements or credit reports are available, use this information to develop estimates of likely nonpayment situations. Another option is to talk to these tenants directly, to understand the status of their operations.
- Will there be collection losses? Does it appear that any tenants will be unable to pay at all? Part of this analysis is based on the size of the deposits held by the landlord; non-payments that extend for several months cannot be fully

offset by deposits. Collection losses will increase further if local pro-tenant legislation makes it difficult to evict tenants.

- What types of leases are in use? Be very clear about whether tenant leases are gross leases, modified gross leases, or net leases (as defined in the preceding chapter). This is essential, since the operating expenses that you pay for will vary, depending on the type of lease.
- What is the state of the economic cycle? When the economy is mired in a downturn, landlords scramble to find the highest-quality tenants in order to avoid payment defaults. This can trigger lowered rents and concession offers to bring in the best tenants.
- How long will units be vacant? Vacancy rates will vary markedly, depending on the economic cycle and the desirability of the property. There will likely be at least a one-month interval between lessees even for a top-notch property at the high point of an economic cycle in a red-hot market. This interval will be substantially longer when the reverse is the case.
- Which expenses are likely to change? Will energy prices spike, causing utility costs to increase? If so, see if any of the regulated utilities providing services to this property have filed for a rate hike.
- What will the debt servicing cost be? Do not rely on the estimated financing provided by the real estate agent. Instead, only use the debt servicing cost as calculated by the firm financing commitment provided to you by your lender.

Tip: One of the few areas in which there is some possibility of reducing expenses is utilities. Investigate the possibility of installing LED lights and low-flow toilets and shower heads, as well as drip irrigation systems, all of which can cut costs. Another option is to cut rental rates and transfer responsibility for electricity usage to the individual tenants; this gives tenants an incentive to cut their electricity usage.

- Will the cost of labor (perhaps for the property manager or maintenance staff) increase? If so, by how much?
- Will insurer losses in the area cause them to increase their insurance rates?
- Will entirely new costs be incurred? Consider all expenses that the current owner has not stated, such as pest control and snow removal. The owner may not be reporting them, because they occur relatively infrequently.
- Will the property's age trigger new expenditures? The building may be due for a major structural renovation, such as a new roof. This concept can also apply to the grounds, such as a parking lot repaving or replacement of the irrigation system. It is exceedingly rare for maintenance expenses to flat-line for years; instead, they continually increase along with the age of the building.

Tip: Inputs to the net operating income calculation are subject to manipulation, since a property owner could elect to accelerate or defer certain expenditures, thereby altering the amount of net operating income. In addition, treat property owner projections of future revenues and expenses with suspicion, since they tend to inflate future revenue while estimating expenses too low, in order to provide you with an excessively rosy picture (and a higher valuation).

EXAMPLE

Henry is contemplating the purchase of a small office building in which space is being leased by four tenants. One tenant has been there for 10 years and seems perfectly satisfied with the arrangement. The second tenant is growing rapidly, and will probably have to move out to find a larger facility when its lease expires in June. Henry assumes that the space will be vacant for two months thereafter, and will cost $20,000 to refurbish. He also expects that any new tenant will want one month of free rent. The third tenant will probably renew when its lease expires in November, but it has already requested $50,000 of facility upgrades as part of the renewal package. Finally, the fourth tenant is in deep financial trouble. Henry expects that it will not be able to make any lease payments, and that he will incur $15,000 of legal costs to evict this party, after which the office space will require $32,000 of refurbishing costs before it can be leased again – while it sits vacant for at least two months. Henry includes these observations in his analysis of the rents likely to be collected from this property within the next year.

It can be useful to include a management fee in your estimates of operating costs for a property, even if you are currently managing it yourself. The reason is that, if you continue to add properties, you will eventually have to hire a property manager – so run the numbers now with this cost included, to see if it still makes sense to acquire the property.

Keep in mind that the net operating income of a property is not the same as its cash flow. The cash flow that a property generates is its net operating income, minus all ongoing debt payments and capital expenditures. Thus, if a property generates $500,000 of net operating income and also requires $350,000 of debt servicing costs and $80,000 of capital expenditures, then the cash flow generated will be $70,000. However, this cash flow figure will be before any income taxes paid. For example, if you pay $25,000 in income taxes related to the property, then the after-tax cash flow from it will be further reduced to $45,000.

Tip: During the early years of property ownership, debt servicing costs are likely to be around 80% of net operating income, plus or minus a few percent.

Gross Potential Income

Of particular interest is the concept of *gross potential income* (GPI). This is the maximum possible amount of income that a property can generate, assuming that it is fully leased out and all tenants are paying on time. This is a useful figure when developing a best-case scenario for a business. With a GPI figure in hand, you can estimate the best possible return on investment, which can put a hard cap on the amount you are willing to spend to acquire a property. For example, if a property's GPI is $2 million and your best estimate of its operating expenses at that level of occupancy is $1.6 million, then the best possible net operating income that it can generate per year is $400,000. If you want to generate at least a 10% return on investment, then the maximum amount you should pay for the property is $4 million (calculated as $400,000 net operating income ÷ 10% return on investment).

Capital Expenditures

We just noted that capital expenditures must be subtracted from net operating income as part of the calculation to derive the cash flows from a property. These expenditures are needed for the replacement or upgrading of the major components of a building. For example, a property may need new windows, air conditioning, a roof, parking lot, appliances, or carpeting. Making these investments is a key part of any long-term investment, since they are needed to preserve the value of the property and provide tenants with good value for their lease payments.

When making capital expenditure estimates, keep in mind that rental properties tend to suffer from unusually high levels of wear and tear, and so will require substantial repairs over time. Even if there is no immediate need to make expenditures in this area, be sure to budget for the funds anyways, so that you will have the cash available when any unexpected expenditures must be made. Realistically, the amount needed for capital expenditures will be on the high end of your estimates, especially for an older property.

> **Tip:** Conduct a detailed walk-through of every prospective property with a contractor who can identify maintenance issues that need to be addressed at once, so that you can budget appropriately for capital expenditures.

> **Tip:** Budget extra for painting and corrosion repairs when a property is located in a humid environment.

Capital expenditures can also be looked upon as an opportunity, especially when the current owner has let a property become run down. Initially spending a substantial amount on a new property acquisition can trigger an immediate jump in its value, and can fully justify an increase in rental rates.

Common Area Maintenance Charges

The costs incurred for a multi-tenant building and which are then passed along to the tenants are known as *common area maintenance (CAM) charges*. These charges are paid by tenants on a proportional basis that is derived from their relative shares of the square footage in the building. Examples of CAM charges are building security, snow removal charges, utilities charged to the common areas, and maintenance performed on the common areas.

CAM charges are typically billed to tenants based on budgeted expenses, with a year-end adjustment to match these billings to the actual expenses incurred. This means that the billing to each tenant will be consistently the same amount for 11 months of the year, with a different billing for the 12th month that is either higher or lower in order to pass through any variances from the budgeted amount.

> **Tip:** When there is a significant change in a CAM expense during the year (usually upward), adjust the monthly billings to tenants at once. Otherwise, there will be tenant protests at year-end, when they receive unusually large CAM billings.

The easiest way to account for CAM charges in your forecasts for a property are to record the expenses by expense type, and then list a subtraction for CAM reimbursement, which is a deduction from the other expenses.

Appraiser Valuation Methods

When a property is being financed with a mortgage, the lender will require that an appraiser issue an appraisal report on it. The reason for doing so is to ensure that the lender does not lend more than the value of the property, so that it can retrieve its funds if it is necessary to foreclose on the property.

When deriving a valuation for a property, an appraiser usually relies on several methods, each of which is derived from different information. Once completed, these methods will probably reveal somewhat different outcomes, which the appraiser then reconciles to arrive at a final valuation figure. The most common methods used are described in the following sub-sections.

Sales Comparison Basis

As the name implies, the sales comparison approach involves developing a price based on a comparison of the targeted property to a variety of similar properties that have sold recently. The resulting sales information will necessarily be in a range of values, since no two properties are entirely alike; they have different floor plans, are in varying conditions, and are situated on different plots of land. A sales comparison will yield better results when there have been a large number of sales recently for similar properties. Clearly, sales comparisons provide better information for condominiums and single-family homes, since there are many more of these units from which comparisons can be made than is the case with large commercial properties.

The highest-quality sales comparison should have the prices from at least three similar property sales that are close to the property you are evaluating. In addition, the ideal comparison properties should be similar in terms of their age, amenities, condition, and size. Given that no comparison properties are exactly alike, an appraiser will make adjustments to account for these differences, resulting in a single estimated value for the target property.

Tip: If there are few completed sales on which to base a sales comparison, consider adding in the sale prices for pending sales. However, treat these prices with caution, since the related transactions may never be completed.

EXAMPLE

Karen wants to acquire a residential property for rental purposes. She has spotted a likely candidate in a nearby neighborhood that costs $550,000 and has 2,800 square feet of finished space, three bedrooms, and three baths. She also collects information about several nearby properties that have sold within the past few months. Their essential information is stated in the following table.

Feature	Target Property	Property A	Property B	Property C
Age	15 years	New	10 years	20 years
Condition	Good	Excellent	Good	Fair
Features	Fiber optic cable	Fiber optic cable	N/A	N/A
Location	Midblock	Corner lot	Midblock	Midblock
Sale date	For sale now	Last month	2 months ago	4 months ago
Price	$550,000	$575,000	$540,000	$520,000

Karen knows that properties are generally valued higher by $1,000 if they have a fiber optic connection. She also knows that corner lots are generally valued about $10,000 higher than midblock properties, and that properties in only fair condition are knocked down by about $30,000, while those in excellent condition experience $15,000 price increases. These adjustments result in the following modifications to the prices of the various properties for comparison purposes:

	Target Property	Property A	Property B	Property C
Price	$550,000	$575,000	$540,000	$520,000
Adjustments	--	-10,000	1,000	31,000
Adjusted price	$550,000	565,000	$541,000	$551,000

The preceding table shows the estimated adjusted price at which the comparison properties would have sold if their features, condition, and location had matched that of the target property. This means that a positive adjustment is made to the price of a comparison property when that property is lacking a feature, condition, or location aspect of the target property, while a negative adjustment is made when the reverse situation is true. These adjusted prices serve as approximations of the value of the target property.

Karen finds that the average adjusted price of the three comparison properties is $552,000, which is slightly higher than the offer price of the target property. Based on this information, she feels that buying at no more than the offer price would be a reasonable investment.

Cost Basis

When there have been few sales in the area recently, an alternative to the sales comparison approach is to derive its replacement cost. This approach is especially useful when you are evaluating a unique property for which any possible sales comparisons would be difficult, as well as for the construction of a proposed new property and any property that has just been completed.

The standard approach for developing a replacement cost for a property is to derive costs for its component parts. The first step is to estimate the value of the land if it were vacant and being employed for its highest and best use. This involves a search for sales of comparable vacant land in the surrounding area. The second step is to estimate the current cost to build the existing building as a new structure. Next, estimate the depreciation[5] of the property and subtract that amount from the cost to build the existing structure; the intent is to derive the cost of the property in its current condition. Then add together your estimated costs for the land and depreciated structure to arrive at the total value of the targeted property.

EXAMPLE

Karen (from the preceding example) estimates that the cost of a comparable vacant midblock location would be $80,000. After conferring with a local building contractor, she concludes that the cost to rebuild the targeted property in its current condition would be $170/square foot. The property is 2,800 square feet, so the total cost of the depreciated structure is $476,000. She adds on the $80,000 value of the land to arrive at a replacement cost of $556,000, which is slightly higher than the list price of the property.

Income Capitalization Basis

An alternative approach is to derive a property's value from the net income that it generates. This method should only be used for the valuation of larger income-generating properties, which means that it is *not* useful for owner-occupied properties where only a portion of the facility is being rented out.

The income capitalization method is based on the direct capitalization formula, which states that the net operating income of a property divided by the capitalization rate equals its value. The formula is as follows:

$$\frac{\text{Net operating income}}{\text{Capitalization rate}} = \text{Property value}$$

---

[5] Depreciation is derived from the normal wear and tear that occurs over time. Depreciation is also derived from the functional obsolescence of a property, as certain features become less desirable for tenants; for example, having just one bathroom in a house would be considered functional obsolescence. Finally, external factors can cause depreciation, such as the decline in value caused by the presence of natural gas in the tap water that was introduced by a local fracking operation.

We addressed the concept of net operating income earlier in this chapter. The *capitalization rate* (or cap rate) is the rate of return that is expected to be generated on a real estate investment. The cap rate is a subjective value that will differ by investor. It can also be derived for the local market by dividing the net operating income for similar properties by the prices at which they sold.

In the formula, the net operating income figure should be stated on a go-forward basis, since historical information is not relevant to a formula that is essentially deriving value from future income.

EXAMPLE

Karen (from the preceding example) conducts an analysis of recent sales in her targeted region, and finds that the cap rate other investors have obtained is 9.5%. She then calculates that the net operating income of the targeted property is $52,000 per year. She plugs this information into the income capitalization formula, as follows:

$52,000 net operating income ÷ 9.5% cap rate = $547,368

Based on this valuation approach, Karen finds that the property value is $547,368.

Though the income capitalization approach quantifies several important performance characteristics of real estate, it does not factor in any potential appreciation of the property, nor does it quantify the risk that the stated amount of net operating income might decline due to tenant turnover or payment defaults. It also does not include the effects of leverage, where a high proportion of debt to invested capital allows you to earn outsized returns. Consequently, it makes sense to incorporate a lower cap rate into the model when there is a good chance of property appreciation, or when leverage opportunities exist, or when tenant turnover levels appear to be low. For example, if Karen had dropped her cap rate to 8.5% in the preceding example, then the derived value of the property would have increased to $611,765. This constitutes a more than $64,000 increase in value, due to a 1% drop in the cap rate.

The Reconciliation of Valuation Methods

Each of the valuation methods just described is a valid approach to valuing a property, and yet each one will probably result in a somewhat different valuation. How can these different numbers be merged into a single valuation figure? Taking a simple average of the three values only works if you assume that each of the methods was equally valid, which is usually not the case. Instead, an appraiser decides which of the methods is the most applicable to the targeted property. To use our ongoing example, Karen has determined that the property is valued at $552,000 using the sales comparison approach, at $556,000 using the cost method, and approximately $547,000 using the income capitalization method, so all values are within a tight range of $9,000. Since she intends to use this property as a real estate investment, rather than an owner-occupied property, she should apply the heaviest weighting to the $547,000 value from the income capitalization method. The cost method seems to be the least relevant, since this is an existing structure, so she throws that figure out. She decides to go with a $548,000 valuation, and makes an offer to the current property owner for that amount.

Summary

The valuation of property is by no means a perfectly refined process, so it is impossible to derive a single number that exactly reflects the existing value of a property. Instead, you will need to understand the different approaches to valuation, and why they will likely result in somewhat different valuation figures. Only a thorough analysis of a targeted property will increase the chances of paying a reasonable price for an investment property.

Chapter 6
Property Acquisition

Introduction

Finding the right property and determining a reasonable price for it are fine, but you still need to close a deal with the current owner. This process is fraught with issues, meaning that many proposed transactions never result in a transfer of ownership. In this chapter, we cover a broad array of issues related to the property acquisition process, including contract essentials, the contents of a purchase agreement, the due diligence process, opening and closing escrow, and selecting the type of entity that will hold title to the property.

The Negotiation Element

One of the ways in which you can earn a return on a real estate investment is through the negotiation process to acquire a property. It may be necessary to drive down the asking price of a property in order to reach (or drop below) the market price or replacement cost of a property. Doing so will generate a better return for you, but will also cut into the return achieved by the seller. An issue to be aware of is that word travels quickly through the real estate community, so it can be harmful to your long-term prospects to drive an unusually hard bargain. Instead, a somewhat more congenial approach can pay off with gaining the inside track on the purchase of other properties in the area.

> **Tip:** It is possible to make a full-price offer, along with a prolonged contingency time frame, which allows you to scour a property for problems, resulting in a steep negotiated drop in the price. Because of the long contingency time frame, the seller cannot cancel escrow and shift to a more reasonable buyer. The result may be a good deal, but will also earn you a poor reputation in the market among real estate agents, making it less likely that any offers for other properties will be accepted.

A good first step in setting up a negotiating strategy is to do the valuation research discussed in the preceding chapter, and determine the highest possible price you are willing to pay that will still generate a reasonable long-term return on investment. In addition, be aware of all risks and opportunities associated with the property, such as, for example, the potential loss of tenants (on the downside) and the potential construction of a hospital nearby (on the upside).

A necessary second step is to learn more about the motivations of the seller. Why is this person selling? By learning more about the needs of the seller, you can structure an offer that meets the individual's needs at a price that makes sense for you. If you have no idea why the person is selling, then expect a tough negotiation, and a greater chance of the sale falling through. Furthermore, if the person does not seem interested in the sales process (such as responding to requests for information), then it is possible that the individual is just testing the market to establish the value of the property, and has no real interest in selling.

> **Tip:** Though it always makes sense to squeeze information from a seller, try not to be overly forthcoming about the reasons for your interest in a property. If you hold forth about your enthusiasm for it, the seller will just hold firm on the asking price.

A final negotiation step is to assemble the facts you want to share with the seller for the negotiation. This means having information about comparable sales in the surrounding area, as well as how you have adjusted the prices to more closely match the target property. In addition, list the quoted cost of the maintenance you will need to have completed as soon as you acquire the property, which is a deduction from the price that you would otherwise pay. This information gives you a rational basis upon which to set a negotiating position, rather than arbitrarily picking a price and arguing randomly to uphold it.

Be aware that most properties on the market are overpriced. Their owners want to wring every possible return from them, and so are willing to wait for an uninformed buyer to accept the asking price. This means that you will have to negotiate hard to bring the price down to a level that makes sense. If the seller is not willing to dicker, then do not bother to prolong the negotiations – just continue searching for alternative properties that represent a better investment value.

Consider using some creative options for meeting the seller's asking price. This can be useful when the seller is totally unwilling to budge on the price. One option is to agree to the price, but only if the seller will complete a specified set of repairs and upgrades prior to handing over the property. Another option is to agree to the price, but only if the seller provides financing at below the market interest rate, so that you will save on the interest expense. Yet another possibility is to agree to the price, but to have the seller pay for the entire amount of the escrow, title, and closing costs. In all three cases, the seller achieves his or her goal of selling at a specific price point, while you achieve an actual out-of-pocket price that is less than this figure.

The basis of any negotiation is the proposed contract that your agent presents to the current owner or the owner's agent. This should be delivered with a time limit, where the counterparty must respond within anywhere from one to three days. The recipient may accept it as is, reject it, let it expire without a response, or make a counteroffer. In the final case, negotiations will be called for, culminating in the presentation of another proposed contract. This process may proceed through a variety of offers or counteroffers before the parties finally agree on the terms of a deal.

The Emotional Hook

When negotiating to acquire a property, it never pays to be emotionally hooked on a specific property. Instead, remember that the property in question is merely an asset from which you hope to generate a return. In order to generate an adequate return, you will have to walk away from a negotiation if the seller is setting a price that is simply too high. This may mean that the negotiations for several consecutive properties fall through; this is the preferred scenario when the other option is entering into a bad deal. Therefore, be patient and do not let your emotions get in the way of achieving a purchase price that works for you.

Contract Essentials

When you want to make an offer to a property owner, your real estate agent prepares a contract, which is then sent to the seller's agent. In this contract, the seller commits to give the buyer title to a property, for which the buyer agrees to pay either in cash or with a combination of cash and a promissory note. There are several concepts associated with a contract that you should be aware of, which are summarized in the following sub-sections.

Contracts with Minors

Many state governments have laws mandating that people must be at least 18 years old before they can enter into a contract. This is done on the grounds that minors do not have the experience or maturity to enter into contracts. Further, minors have the right to cancel most contracts that they have entered into with an adult. Conversely, an adult does not have this right when the counterparty to a contract is a minor. This right of cancellation is useful for cancelling contracts that are disadvantageous to a minor. A minor can cancel a contract in several ways, including through the use of a written notification, a verbal statement, or via his or her conduct.

At the point when a minor cancels a contract, the minor must return any consideration received from the adult, in the condition it is in at that time. This can mean that the value of the consideration will have declined by the time it is returned, creating a loss for the adult. However, if the loss in value was intentional or due to gross negligence by the minor, then the full value of the consideration must be returned. Full value of the consideration must also be returned when a minor misrepresents his or her age to the adult.

Conversely, an adult participating in a contract that has been cancelled must return any consideration received from the minor; if the consideration has declined in value or been sold, then the adult must return the cash equivalent of its value.

If a minor does not cancel a contract by the time he or she becomes an adult, then the contract is considered to have been accepted. This means that the former minor is now bound by the contract.

Contracts with Mentally Incompetent Individuals

When mentally incompetent people enter into a contract, they are not bound to it, on the grounds that they may not understand the consequences of the contract on them. To be released from the terms of a contract, a person must have been legally insane when he or she entered into it. Legal insanity is present when a person cannot understand the nature of a transaction.

When a court has judged a person to be insane, then any contract entered into by that person is void. Only the person's court-appointed guardian then has the authority to enter into contracts on behalf of the individual. If there has been no formal court judgment that a person is insane, but the person suffers from a mental impairment, then the individual can void any contract that he or she enters into. When the other party to a contract was not aware that a person was insane and the contract is voided, then the other party is due full restitution for any consideration given.

The Offer

The formation of a contract begins with one party making an offer to another party. This is usually the result of negotiations back and forth, after which one person (the offeror) makes an offer to the other party (the offeree). This offer states the terms under which the offeror is willing to enter into a contract with the offeree. The offer is not considered effective until it is received by the offeree.

The terms of the offer must be sufficiently clear that the offeree can decide whether to accept it. For this to be the case, the offer must identify the parties, the subject matter, the quantity and price, the time of performance, and the amount to be paid. If any of these terms are indefinite, a court can insert a missing term, as long as the term is implied in the contract. For example, a price can be implied when there is an active market from which it can be derived. It is also possible to imply the time of performance. However, it is not usually possible to imply the subject matter of a contract when the item is unique, such as the design and construction of a patio for a homeowner.

Offer Terminations

There are several ways in which an offer can be terminated. One method is for the offeror to withdraw the offer at any time prior to when the offeree accepts it. This approach is effective as soon as the offeree receives it. Another approach to offer termination is for the offeree to reject it. Once this rejection notice has been received by the offeror, the offeree cannot subsequently accept the offer. In a real estate transaction, the most efficient way to arrange for an offer termination is to state within the offer the date on which the offer will automatically terminate.

Offer Acceptance

An offer can only be validly accepted in an unequivocal manner. This means that a statement of acceptance can have only one possible meaning, without any exceptions or conditions. For example, Angie offers to sell an investment property to Victoria for $1,000,000, to which the response is "I think I'd like to buy it, but let me think about it." This response constitutes hedging, and so cannot be construed as an acceptance.

Note: As long as an emailed acceptance to an offer has been made in an unequivocal manner, it is a valid acceptance of the offer.

An offer is only considered to have been accepted when the offeree accepts it without any attempt to modify the offer. When a modification is proposed, this constitutes a counteroffer, and so cancels the original offer. For example, a property owner offers to sell an apartment building for $1,500,000, which the offeree accepts under the provision that the seller includes a five-year warranty on the heating system. The demand for a warranty creates a counteroffer, and so voids the original offer.

An offer is not assumed to have been accepted when the offeree does not respond. This keeps an offeree from being held liable through inaction. For example, an offer to sell the offeree a property for $350,000 by Saturday unless the offeror hears otherwise does not constitute a valid acceptance.

An offer is assumed to have been accepted when the offeree issues an acceptance by an authorized mode of communication, even if the acceptance is then lost in transmission. This *mailbox rule* can be altered by changing the terms of an offer to state that acceptance occurs when the offeror receives the acceptance.

Consideration

A contract is only enforceable when it involves *consideration*, which is something of legal value that is given in exchange for a promise. For example, consideration can involve the payment of cash, the transfer of property, or the promise not to engage in some type of action. Consideration has been given when (for example) one party pays another party $10,000 to forbear from engaging in a lawsuit (which involves the payment of cash in exchange for a promise not to do something).

Written Contract

Any contract for the transfer of property must be in writing, including complete documentation of all terms and conditions. A high level of documentation is needed in order to be clear about what is and is not included in a sale transaction. For example, if the furniture in a rental property is to be included in a sale, then this requirement must be documented. Otherwise, the seller has no obligation to transfer the furniture. In addition, a contract with a real estate agent should be in writing, as should any agreement to lease property for more than one year.

Contents of the Purchase Agreement

The purchase agreement is used to buy and sell real estate. It contains a number of clauses that identify the buyer and seller, describe the property, the conditions that must be met prior to closing, and how the transaction will be financed. Also, it notes the circumstances under which the agreement can be terminated.

Most of the text included in a purchase agreement is standardized (though there is no single standardized agreement used by the entire industry). When filling out a purchase agreement, be sure to make an entry in every blank field in the agreement, put a line through all text that you do not want, and initial every change. The counterparty should also initial these changes, which indicates that both parties agree to the stated terms.

The terms included in a purchase agreement will vary by real estate market. Your real estate agent can provide advice regarding which terms are considered acceptable in the market where you want to make a purchase. In particular, the following topics will need to be addressed in the agreement.

Earnest Money Deposit

This is a deposit made to a seller that represents a buyer's good faith to buy a property. The money gives the buyer extra time to obtain financing and conduct a title search, property appraisals, and inspections prior to closing. It frequently makes sense to offer a substantial deposit, which indicates that you are serious about closing a deal. This deposit is never made to the seller, but rather to the seller's agent or an escrow company. You should require that the earnest money be placed in an insured, interest-bearing trust account, from which you are credited with any interest earned.

> **Tip:** Monitor your compliance with the purchase agreement, since not doing so or not cancelling the agreement by the specified date will result in the forfeiture of your earnest money deposit. Any oral agreement to extend the term of the agreement is not sufficient; it must be in writing, or you will be in danger of losing the deposit. This forfeiture represents damages paid to the seller for your nonperformance.

Assignment of Interests

A useful clause to include in a purchase agreement is an assignment of interests clause. This clause transfers your rights or duties as stated in the agreement. An easy way to include an assignment is simply to state the name of the purchasing entity in the contract, as well as the words "or assignee". For example, the purchasing entity could be "Murchison Properties LLC or assignee".

Having an assignment clause is a good outlet in case you do not want to complete a transaction (perhaps because a better opportunity came along) and it is too late to recover your earnest money. In this case, you can sell your interest to a third party, thereby allowing you to escape from the deal with your funds intact.

An assignment is most useful in a market where property prices are increasing at a blistering pace. When this is the case, it may be possible to generate a profit simply by selling your interest in the contract to a third party. For example, you could enter into an agreement with a developer to buy a home at a certain fixed price that will not be completed for another year, and then sell your interest to another buyer at an increased price, thereby generating a profit without ever owning the property.

Developers do not always allow an assignment of rights, since they are aware of how properties can be flipped for an immediate profit. If so, you will need to complete the initial sale (along with paying the commission and other fees), and then sell the property to a third party (while incurring the commission and other fees).

Closing Date

The proposed closing date stated in the agreement should be long enough to cover the likely time period required to obtain financing, as well as the activities that must be completed in order to investigate all due diligence items. When you expect difficulties in either of these areas, push for a more distant closing date, so that all required items can be completed. Insisting on a lengthy closing period can cause friction with the seller, who may be motivated to sell quickly. A seller may also object to a distant closing date, based on prior experience with hard-nosed buyers that use the extra time to bargain for a lower price or more concessions. A possible solution is to set a worst-case closing date, which you have the option to accelerate if you complete all required tasks earlier than expected.

> **Tip:** In a hot market where there are many sale transactions, appraisers may have substantial backlogs, in which case your loan application will be delayed – which in turn will extend the closing date.

Contingencies

Either party may want to include contingency clauses in the contract. These clauses identify conditions that must be met prior to the closing date. If the contingencies are not addressed, then the sale transaction is never finalized. Contingencies are more commonly imposed by the buyer, who needs them to keep from acquiring a property that does not meet his or her requirements. In effect, a contingency mitigates the risk of the buyer. Common contingencies are as follows:

- An appraisal report must determine that the property value is equal to or greater than the purchase price of the property.
- The buyer has a fixed amount of time in which to conduct a thorough inspection of the property. The outcome of this analysis can then be used to terminate the deal, adjust the purchase price, or convince the seller to complete a variety of repairs.
- The buyer must be able to obtain financing to complete the purchase.
- The property must have a marketable title, which is a title that is free from reasonable doubt or any sort of threat of litigation.
- The seller provides access to the property's accounting records, so that the buyer can confirm that its revenues and expenses were as represented.

A common contingency is that the buyer must secure financing prior to the closing date. Or, the buyer might require 15 days in which to conduct an inspection of the property.

When a specified contingency has been resolved, the property sale can no longer be cancelled because of that specific contingency. Alternatively, whichever party is benefiting from a contingency can choose to waive it. The only other outcome is that the contingent condition fails, in which case the benefiting party no longer has an obligation to perform. For example, if there is a funding contingency and the buyer is unable to secure the necessary funding, then the buyer can walk away from the contract, along with his earnest money deposit.

Personal Property

Part of the agreement should itemize the assets that will be included in the sale. These assets may comprise a substantial part of the value, depending on the situation, as it includes furniture and fixtures, maintenance supplies, and appliances. This is more of an issue in larger properties.

Vacant Property

If you intend to shut down the property for a period of time in order to conduct renovation activities, you can require the current owner to deliver the property without tenants. This puts the onus on the seller of clearing the property prior to the sale date. This clause only arises when tenants are not currently on long-term leases.

Escrow Extension

It is always useful to include an escrow (as explained next) extension in the agreement. This clause should allow for a modest extension of a few weeks at no cost due to delays that are beyond the buyer's control. This clause is intended to improve the odds that the purchase will be completed.

Opening Escrow

The mutual agreement of the parties to a contract is merely the opening act in the process of acquiring a property. The next step is opening escrow, where the real estate agent opens an escrow account at an independent third party and deposits your earnest money deposit there. This escrow account is managed by an escrow agent in order to hold valuables on behalf of the parties until specific conditions are met. Depending on the situation, the escrow agent could be a title company that specializes in real estate, a bank, or perhaps an attorney. The agent acts as a neutral third party that collects the necessary money and documents required for the closing process, including the earnest money payment, the loan documents, and the signed deed.

The escrow agent will prepare a set of escrow instructions that define the events and conditions that must take place, and the manner in which the agent shall deliver or release to the beneficiary of the escrow the assets, documents, and/or money held in escrow. These instructions are derived from the terms stated in the purchase agreement. You should review these instructions carefully before signing off on them, because the agent will rely on this document when deciding how to handle any disputes between the parties. If an action is not allowed in the instructions, the buyer and seller will need to mutually present the agent with a change order that allows the action.

The next step is to obtain a title report from the title company. This report verifies that title to the property is clear – that is, that there are no liens on the property and no one other than the seller has a claim to any part of it. It will also show any encumbrances against the property, such as easements or restrictions, that could limit how the property is used. If there are any problems with the title, the seller will have to fix them prior to the sale date. If the title report contains unacceptable items, the buyer can cancel the purchase.

The escrow agent is responsible for tracking all contingencies listed in the purchase agreement, as well as for following the instructions received from the buyer and seller in regard to these items. Since contingencies can be used by the benefiting party to cancel a purchase, they are central to completing an acquisition. Consequently, the agent needs to keep track of the expiration date for each contingency and determine whether it has been satisfied, rejected, or waived.

Tip: If you have a contingency option and plan to reject it, you must notify the escrow agent of this fact in writing, and as soon as possible.

Due Diligence

Once the current property owner accepts your purchase offer, the next step in the acquisition process is due diligence, where you bring in inspectors to evaluate the condition of the property. Due diligence spans the time period between the seller's acceptance of the purchase agreement and the close of escrow.

Tip: Do not let the seller impose any limitations on access to the property that will prevent you from conducting a thorough set of inspections. If the seller persists in doing so, this is a major red flag that there may be a problem with the property.

This is a critical step, because the condition of the property might not be quite what the seller had represented it to be. If you find deficiencies, this can result in further negotiations to determine who will make the necessary repairs, and who will pay for them. The following activities are useful due diligence actions:

- *Environmental inspection.* Have an environmental inspection conducted to check for toxins in the property, such as mold, radon gas, and asbestos. A Phase I Environmental Report is required for commercial and larger residential properties. If a problem is noted in a Phase I report, remediation may be so expensive that it is best to cancel the purchase.
- *Flood report.* See if the property is located in a flood plain. This is a critical item, since it can be impossible to obtain a mortgage if a property is subject to excessive flooding.
- *Geologic report.* If the area is located in an earthquake zone, obtain a geologic report to assess the risk of damage to the property in the event of an earthquake.
- *Land survey.* Verify the boundaries of the property. This is more of an issue in rural areas, where boundaries tend to be more suspect.
- *Pest inspection.* Have a pest inspection conducted to ensure that the property does not have termites, carpenter ants, or other pests such as roaches or rats. The inspectors should also report on any property damage caused by these

pests. Look in particular for recommendations to replace compromised structural elements, which can be extremely expensive.

- *Structural inspection.* This review focuses on a wide range of issues, including structural integrity, crawl spaces, the roof, plumbing systems, electrical systems, smoke detectors, windows, weatherproofing, and illegal construction.

Tip: Accompany the inspectors as they review the property. Doing so gives you first-hand knowledge of any issues found.

INSPECTION RED FLAGS

When conducting inspections, there are several issues that can be indicators of much larger problems that will require an in-depth investigation. You should watch out for cracks anywhere, including cracks in the foundation, walls, door frames, and chimneys. Also look out for soft spots in the flooring that can be indicative of termite damage or rotted wood. Also look for poor drainage that can cause cracked or bulging retaining walls. Major indicators of water leaks are ceiling or wall stains, or a moldy smell.

Be particularly wary of any property whose tenants use petroleum solvents, such as dry cleaners and manufacturers. The associated environmental remediation can be exceedingly expensive.

A useful additional inspection is by your architectural advisor. This person can make suggestions for how to improve the property, which can be useful for providing value to tenants that can result in increased rents.

Tip: Do not try to save money by conducting your own inspections, unless you are a licensed professional in the areas being inspected. Missing a major issue during inspection due to your own lack of knowledge could turn out to have very expensive consequences.

A good reason to use professional inspectors is that their inspection reports can then be used as the basis for negotiations with the seller, either to have that party pay for the repairs, or to lower the price by the amount of the projected repair cost.

Tip: If you are buying the property "as is," then there will be no possibility of negotiating any seller concessions.

This is your last chance to conduct a deep dive on the seller's financial records for the property. This means conducting a detailed examination of the seller's reported revenue and expenses for the property. Even if this inspection does not uncover any problems, it may provide clues for possible revenue increases or expense reductions after you have taken possession of the property.

> **Tip:** Look for discrepancies between the pro forma operating statement supplied by the seller during your initial investigation and the actual revenue and expense information.

It is essential to review the seller's lease agreements. This means verifying lease expiration dates, security deposits, and lease rates. Also, obtain a written statement from the seller that there are no undisclosed side agreements with tenants regarding concessions, renewal options, or rental rates.

It is also useful to verify that all supporting documentation is available for each tenant. This means checking to see if their rental application, current lease agreement, maintenance work orders, legal notices, and other correspondence is on file.

Another area of investigation is the contracts the property has with service providers, such as pest control, lawn care, and property maintenance. This investigation can be useful for comparing rates to what you are paying to the service providers of your other properties, possibly resulting in some changes to obtain lower-cost services.

If the property is required to have a business license or other permits, verify that these licenses and permits are up-to-date. Once you officially obtain title to the property, you will need to notify the relevant government agencies of the change of ownership.

A useful investigation is to obtain the seller's history of loss claims under its insurance policies. This history is useful not only for learning more about the loss history of the property, but also to provide your insurance agent with information for compiling bids from insurance carriers for coverage, once you take over the property.

Disclosure Requirements

Many states require that the seller of a smaller residential rental property disclose to the seller in writing all known mechanical and structural deficiencies (known as a transfer disclosure statement). If the seller does not disclose something, the buyer can sue for damages in the amount of any repair or replacement costs related to the undisclosed item.

A seller may put a property up for sale "as is," so that the buyer is committing to acquire the property in its current condition, irrespective of any repair issues that may be present. The seller still needs to supply a transfer disclosure statement, if the state government mandates it.

> **Tip:** Any property offered for sale on an "as is" basis is generally to be avoided, on the grounds that there may be substantial issues with the property that will require a major investment to correct.

The Entity That Will Hold Title

Before taking ownership of a property, you should consider the nature of the entity that will hold title to the property, since there are a variety of taxation and risk management issues that vary by entity type. In the following sub-sections, we provide a summary of the characteristics of the entity types most commonly used to hold title to a property.

Sole Proprietorship

A sole proprietorship is a business that is not incorporated; instead, it is merely an extension of the person who owns it. This means that the owner is entitled to the entire net worth of the business, and is personally liable for its debts. The business has no legal existence in the absence of the owner. A sole proprietorship is created when a property title is vested in your name.

The advantages of a sole proprietorship are:

- *Simple to organize.* The initial organization of the business is quite simple. At most, the owner might reserve a business name with the secretary of state. It is also quite easy to upgrade to other forms of organization.
- *Lower costs.* The accounting costs associated with a sole proprietorship tend to be quite low, since it is not necessary to maintain a separate set of books.
- *Simple tax filings.* The owner does not have to file a separate income tax return for the business. Instead, the results of the business are listed on a separate schedule of the individual income tax return (Form 1040).
- *Complete control.* There is only one owner, who has absolute control over the direction of the property.
- *Withdrawals.* There is no tax effect when the owner transfers money to the business or removes money from it.

The disadvantages of a sole proprietorship are:

- *Unlimited liability.* The chief disadvantage is that the owner is entirely liable for any losses incurred by the property, with no limitation. For example, the owner may invest $1,000 in a real estate venture, which then incurs net obligations of $100,000. The owner is personally liable for the entire $100,000. An adequate amount of liability insurance and risk management practices can mitigate this concern.
- *No tax advantages.* This approach provides no tax advantages. Instead, all income and expenses associated with a property appear on the owner's individual tax return.
- *No outside equity.* The only provider of equity to the business is the sole owner. Funding usually comes from personal savings and debt for which the owner is liable. For a large increase in capital, the owner would likely need to use a different organizational structure that would admit multiple owners.

- *Marriage concerns*. Getting married after acquiring property presents the danger that the spouse could have a legal interest in the property, which may cause a significant loss of wealth in the event of a divorce.

The unlimited liability aspect of the sole proprietorship and the inability to bring in additional investors tends to limit its use to smaller property investments that require reduced levels of funding.

Partnership

A partnership is a form of business organization to which the owners have made some sort of contribution (such as money, labor, or property) and from which they share in the resulting profits and losses. This is a useful form of organization for property investments, especially when the partners bring a variety of relevant skills to the business. For example, a partnership could include a real estate broker, an appraiser, a property manager, and a financial analyst. Alternatively, one partner could provide the bulk of the needed funds, and leaves the active property investment activities to other partners who are more skilled in this area.

In a general partnership, the partners have unlimited personal liability for the actions of the business; this means that any one partner can be held liable for the actions of the other partners. In a limited partnership, a general partner runs the business and has unlimited liabilities, while a number of limited partners are not involved in business operations, and are only at risk for the amount they invested in the partnership. Given the minimal downside risk, limited partnerships are a quite popular vehicle for property investments.

The owners of a partnership have invested their own funds and time in the business, and share proportionally in any profits earned by it, which are passed through to them. Thus, the partnership itself does not pay any income taxes; instead, income and losses are passed through to the partners, who are responsible for these payments, based on their own personal income tax brackets.

It can be difficult to sell your interest in a partnership, so it is best to address this issue in a partnership agreement that requires the other partners to buy you out using a predetermined valuation formula.

The advantages of a partnership are:

- *Source of capital*. With many partners, a business has a much richer source of capital than would be the case for a sole proprietorship.
- *Classes of ownership*. There can be more than one class of partnership interests.
- *Specialization*. If there is more than one general partner, it is possible for multiple people with diverse skill sets to run a business, which can enhance its overall performance. In general, this may mean that there is more expertise within the business.
- *Special allocations*. The partnership agreement can state special partner allocations that differ from the respective ownership interests of the partners.

- *Pass-through*. Income, losses and credits are passed through to the partners for taxation purposes.

The disadvantages of a partnership are:

- *Unlimited liability*. The partners have unlimited personal liability for the obligations of the partnership, as was the case with a sole proprietorship. This is a *joint and several liability*, which means that creditors can pursue a single general partner for the obligations of the entire business.
- *Taxed on undistributed earnings*. The partners are taxed on the current earnings of the partnership, even if those earnings are not distributed to them. This can cause problems when the partnership needs to retain the cash to support operations, while the partners need it to pay taxes.
- *Multiple tax filings*. When the partnership spans multiple states, partners may have to file individual state income tax returns in all of those states.

Corporation

A C corporation uses a corporate structure that is taxed directly, rather than passing income through to its owners for taxation purposes. This tax structure is useful, in that the corporate tax rate is substantially less than the tax rate charged to high-income individuals. Since less cash is paid to the government, a corporation has more cash available for other purposes, such as reinvesting profits in the business. Also, since it has a corporate structure, its owners do not incur any liabilities taken on by the corporation, and so are not liable to its creditors. Another benefit is that a corporation can survive its owners, persisting as new owners take the place of the old ones. Yet another advantage is that the entity can issue a variety of types of stock, such as several classes of preferred stock, which allows it to raise money more easily than other legal forms of business. Furthermore, anyone can be a shareholder, including nonresident aliens, trusts, estates, another C corporation, and so forth. An essential advantage of a corporation is the free transferability of interests, where a shareholder's interest in the corporation (a stock certificate) can be sold to another party.

The single largest complaint about the C corporation is the concept of double taxation. In essence, the corporation is taxed on its earnings, while its shareholders are taxed again when they receive dividends from the corporation. This issue can be reduced when shareholders are also employees, by paying them a salary instead of dividends (though doing so will incur payroll taxes).

A corporation is formed by registering with the secretary of state's office for the applicable state, and issuing stock certificates to its owners. The shareholders then elect a board of directors, which governs the entity in their stead. The board hires a management team, which runs the business for them. The corporate secretary is also responsible for filing an annual report with the secretary of state's office for as long as the entity remains in business.

The advantages of a C corporation are:

- *Liability shield*. Shareholders are not liable for the obligations of the corporation.
- *Fringe benefits*. It can deduct the cost of any fringe benefits it pays to any shareholders who are also employees. Examples of these benefits are medical insurance, life insurance, and disability insurance.
- *Multiple stock classes*. It can issue multiple classes of stock in order to attract investors with differing requirements.
- *Transferable shares*. Depending on whether shares are restricted, it is relatively easy for parties to buy and sell shares in a corporation.

The main disadvantage of a C corporation is double taxation, where its earnings are taxed when earned, while any dividends are taxable to the receiving shareholders. This problem is solved by the S corporation, where all items of income, deduction, credit, gain, and loss pass directly through to the entity's shareholders, who then pay all taxes on their own income tax returns. An additional benefit is that the shareholders gain protection from the creditors of the corporation, as would be the case with a C corporation.

Limited Liability Company

A limited liability company (LLC) is a business entity that provides its owners (known as members[6]) with the limited liability protection of a corporation, while allowing earnings to pass through to the members for tax purposes. Thus, an LLC combines the best features of a corporation and a partnership while not being classified as either one; as such, it is a commonly-used entity for holding title. An LLC is created by state statute, and is usually taxable as a partnership under federal tax law. However, LLC law may differ by state, and may not exist at all in some states, which presents a concern that the liability protections afforded by this structure may not be valid in certain states.

An LLC has a clear advantage over a C corporation in the matter of compensation. The IRS can disallow a salary paid to a shareholder as being unreasonable compensation, so that it is instead taxed as a dividend. This is not the case with an LLC, where the IRS does not care if a member is paid via a distributive share of income or via a salary.

The advantages of a limited liability company are:

- *Active participation*. Members can actively participate in the management of the business, which is not the case with a limited partnership. This means that there is no need to designate a general partner to run the business.

---

[6] A member is an individual or entity holding a membership interest in an LLC. Members are the owners of an LLC, like shareholders are the owners of a corporation. Initial members are admitted at the time of formation. Additional members may be admitted based on the conditions set forth in the operating agreement.

- *Limited liability.* Members are not personally liable for the debts of the business, which is not the case with a partnership.
- *Earnings pass-through.* If the entity is taxed as a partnership, then its earnings are passed through to its members.
- *Unique rights.* Special rights can be set up to favor some members over others in the allocation of taxable income and losses. In addition, these rights can be adjusted by altering the LLC's operating agreement.
- *Multiple classes of stock.* An LLC can issue multiple classes of stock, which gives it the opportunity to provide different rights to different groups of shareholders.

The disadvantages of a limited liability company are:

- *State specific.* The laws concerning LLCs are at the state level, and there are differences between state laws (or there are no laws at all). A possible outcome is that an LLC established in one state may lose its liability protection if it operates in another state that has no LLC statute, or one with different laws.
- *Restrictions on use.* Some states specifically restrict the types of businesses that can use the LLC structure.

Concurrent Ownership

Several people may own real property, which is known as concurrent ownership. There are several variations on the concept, which are noted below:

- *Joint tenancy.* This is co-ownership with a right of survivorship, which is most commonly associated with married couples. Thus, if one co-owner dies, full ownership of the property passes to the surviving joint tenant. The surviving tenant receives a stepped-up basis on the deceased tenant's portion of the property, which represents a massive tax benefit. This property vesting occurs without having to go through probate court. Joint tenancy is only created when both parties take ownership of a property at the same time and in equal amounts. A major concern is that any joint tenant can sell or encumber his or her portion of a property without obtaining the consent of the other owner(s).

EXAMPLE

Mark and Andrea purchase a property for $400,000 as joint tenants. Mark dies 20 years later, at which point the property is appraised at $600,000. The new adjusted basis for Andrea, the surviving joint tenant, is $500,000 (calculated as her original basis of $200,000, plus Mark's $300,000 stepped-up share of the property). If Andrea were to then sell the property for its appraised value of $600,000, her increased basis would result in a taxable gain of only $100,000.

- *Tenancy in common*. This is co-ownership where each party's ownership interest passes to that person's estate, rather than to the co-owner. Under this arrangement, the owning parties can own differing percentages of a property, and dispose of their interests at any time without the approval of the other owners. A fractionalized interest in real estate is usually structured to be a tenancy in common. A potential problem with tenancy in common is that a co-owner sells to an incompatible party. Another issue is that the bankruptcy of one owner can lead to the forced sale of the property in order to satisfy the claims of that owner's creditors. Also, there may be differences of opinion among the owners about how a property should be managed.

Closing the Transaction

A property purchase is completed only after escrow has been closed. It can require a substantial effort by many parties to ensure that all terms of the deal have been settled, and all terms of the escrow instructions and purchase agreement have been fulfilled. Once this has occurred, the escrow officer can close the transaction. This means that the parties sign all relevant documents, after which funds are transferred among the various parties.

> **Tip:** It pays to stay on top of all open items, constantly nagging the responsible parties to complete their assigned tasks. Otherwise, a key item may not be completed by the closing date, requiring you to extend the escrow period.

Shortly before the close of escrow, the buyer and seller will be sent an estimated closing statement, in which is listed all charges associated with the transaction. Be sure to review it in detail, since this is your last chance to protest any charges that you feel may have been made in error. The statement also indicates the additional cash that the buyer must deposit (usually via a cashier's check or a wire transfer) – which must be completed before escrow can close.

The closing statement contains several issues that may require some negotiation between the buyer and seller. The following bullet points contain the issues more likely to require your attention:

- *Appraisal fee*. The buyer pays the fee charged by an appraiser to develop an appraisal for the property in question.
- *Broker's commission*. The seller normally pays the entire amount of the broker's commission.
- *Escrow fees*. The buyer and seller usually pay an equal share of the escrow fees.
- *Lender's title policy*. The buyer pays for the title insurance that guarantees to the lender that the title is valid.
- *Loan commitment fee*. The buyer pays the loan commitment fee charged by the lender.

- *Loan origination fee.* The buyer pays the loan origination fee charged by the lender.
- *Loan prepayment penalty.* The seller pays for any loan prepayment fee associated with paying off the seller's mortgage early.
- *Property tax apportionment.* The seller might have already paid property taxes for the entire year, in which case the buyer should pay the seller that portion of these taxes that is attributable to the buyer's ownership period.
- *Seller's title policy.* The seller pays for the title insurance that guarantees to the buyer that the title is valid.
- *Transfer tax.* The seller normally pays the transfer tax. This is a charge levied on the transfer of title to property from one party to another.

It is extremely likely that *title insurance* will be required as part of the closing. This insurance is a form of indemnity insurance that protects lenders and property purchasers from financial loss sustained from defects in the title to a property. For example, if someone other than a property's legal owner were to fraudulently sell the property, the legal owner could then reclaim the property, forcing the buyer to relinquish it. Title insurance compensates the buyer for this loss. The seller may provide it to the buyer, or a mortgage lender will require it in order to be protected from the potential loss of its loan collateral (the property).

A mortgage lender will insist that you maintain property insurance on an acquired property. Otherwise, damage to the property reduces the value of the lender's collateral. Consequently, you will need to obtain a certificate of insurance from a property insurer, and forward it to the escrow officer.

Tip: Investigate the price of property insurance early in the due diligence process, so that you can terminate other investigations and back out of the deal if the cost of the insurance is too high. Also, the insurer may inspect the property and demand that certain upgrades or maintenance be performed before it will provide coverage – the cost of which can also cause you to terminate the transaction.

Tip: Verify in writing that your new property insurance is in force prior to the closing. Otherwise, there is a risk that damage will occur immediately thereafter, and you will not have insurance coverage for it.

Just prior to the closing, walk through the property to ensure that all appliances, fixtures, and so forth that are mandated by the purchase agreement are still there. If not, contact the seller at once and ensure that these items are returned.

After all documents have been signed and funds paid, the escrow agent will notify the county recorder to record the associated property deed. Once the deed has been recorded, this finalizes the transaction.

Once the closing has been completed, the escrow agent completes the Form 1099-S, *Proceeds from Real Estate Transactions*, to report the sale or exchange of real estate to the Internal Revenue Service. Alternatively, the brokers may be required to file this report.

Tip: Keep a copy of the closing statement in a safe place, such as a safe deposit box, since the information in it identifies your cost basis in the property. This information will be needed when you eventually sell the property, in order to calculate the amount of any capital gain or loss.

Transfer of Ownership

Once you take ownership of a property, there are a few tasks to complete within the first few days of ownership. One is to contact the government agencies that have issued a business license or other permits to the property, to transfer ownership information on the license and permits.

Another task is to contact all electricity, water, natural gas, trash collection, and Internet providers – essentially, all utilities – and have them switch the billing over to the entity that now owns the property. Ideally, the changeover should be as of the escrow closing date. If the switchover can be arranged as of this date, it will not be necessary to prorate any billings between the new and former owners.

Another essential task is to take possession of all keys that provide access to the property. It may be prudent to change all the locks, to guard against any third parties who might have copies of the existing keys.

A final issue is to meet with all tenants and give them your contact information. Doing so not only keeps them from bothering the prior owner, but also allows you to immediately start building relations with tenants who may decide to continue leasing from you for many years to come.

Summary

There are many boxes to check off before you can complete an acquisition. Chief among these items is the due diligence process. Spend as much time (and money) as needed to ensure that all key issues are found and discussed with the seller. Otherwise, you may decide to purchase a property that has a large number of expensive undisclosed problems – quite possibly resulting in no prospect of ever turning a profit on the property.

Chapter 7
Property Management

Introduction

You've survived the minefield of locating the right property, financing it, and closing a deal. Now for the hard part – managing it. In this chapter, we cover many aspects of property management, including whether you should manage properties yourself, which rental policies to set, screening applicants, updating the property, and managing risk. Paying attention to every one of these issues is essential, since the profits generated from a property are likely to be razor-thin during your first few years of ownership. A slip-up anywhere could cost you.

Managing a Property Yourself

There are many aspects to renting a property, some of which you may not be overly interested in performing. Perhaps you are less interested in conducting routine maintenance, or dealing with tenants, or advertising for new ones. Nonetheless, it can be worthwhile to understand the advantages of managing a property yourself. First, there will be no property management fee. This is a significant issue, since property managers can soak up a large part of the revenues generated by a property. Also, conducting your own maintenance can eliminate substantial contractor fees. These two savings can be the difference between a marginally profitable property and one that spins off large amounts of cash.

There is a downside to managing a property yourself, which is the amount of time required. When you are spending every waking moment managing property, there is no time left to scout for additional property acquisitions. This means that direct management will necessarily limit the size of your real estate empire. In addition, responding on short notice to tenant issues can interfere with your day job or require you to get up in the middle of the night. Furthermore, the amount of time saved by managing a property directly may not offset your loss of income from the hours that could have been spent on other activities. Finally, direct management can mean that you cannot take any time off for vacations, since you will need to be available to handle any issues that may arise. For these reasons, many investors elect to manage their first one or two properties directly, after which they decide to hand off all operational issues to others and concentrate on expanding their ownership interests.

> **Tip:** It can make sense to use a property management company, if only because they can obtain volume discounts from contractors for such activities as mowing and general maintenance.

A further consideration when deciding whether to directly manage a property is whether you are personally suited to engaging in this type of work. Those who are more outgoing and positive by nature will have an easier time dealing with tenants, who may sometimes be angry about a problem with their rental space. Directly handling maintenance issues calls for particular electrical, plumbing, heating, carpentry, and other skills that few people have. Further, are you willing to keep track of rental agreements and the accounting associated with them? While you may be suited in some respects, it is unlikely that you are the perfect hands-on landlord – in which case you should outsource those aspects of the job that make you most uncomfortable.

A particular concern when it comes to property management is being able to engage in robust discussions (argue) with tenants. This is a necessary job requirement, since tenants must be held to the lease agreements that they signed. This means avoiding being manipulated by a tenant into making more expensive upgrades than are strictly required, as well as ensuring that payments are made on time and verifying that tenants are not causing undue damage to the property. If you do not have such a personality, then hiring a property manager will be mandatory.

Outsourcing Work

The preceding discussion should make it clear that at least some portion of the property management work will probably need to be outsourced. The biggest decision is whether to shift overall management to a property management firm. These businesses take responsibility for every aspect of the ongoing management of a property. They deal with tenants on your behalf, locate replacement tenants, and fix maintenance issues. Given their importance, spend a substantial amount of time locating a property management firm that has extensive experience with the types of property you own (such as condos or retail stores) and which is already managing properties in your area. When interviewing the firm, consider the following points:

- Ascertain how they calculate their management fee. The best arrangement is as a percentage of the collected income from a property, rather than a fixed fee. The percentage-basis fee motivates the firm to collect all rents from tenants.
- Ascertain whether the firm passes through the discounts it receives from suppliers for services performed on your property, or whether they retain these amounts and charge you full price.
- Ascertain whether the firm will set up a separate bank account for the transactions associated with your property, rather than using a single master account for all of its properties.
- Collect references for property owners with the same types of property that you own, and who have been with the property management firm for several years.
- Determine whether the assigned property manager is certified as a Certified Property Manager, Accredited Residential Manager, or Accredited Commercial Manager.
- Discuss the types of property they already manage. Verify that they have substantial experience with your types of property.

- Talk to the person who will have direct responsibility for your properties, to see if he or she has a sufficient level of experience.
- Verify that the firm has a current property manager's license (which depends on the requirements of the applicable state government). Contact the applicable government agency to see if any complaints have been filed against the firm.
- Verify that the firm has a fidelity bond, which provides you with coverage if anyone at the firm steals the rental payments that they are collecting on your behalf.
- Verify that the firm has current insurance policies for professional liability, automobile liability, and general liability.

After selecting a property management firm, it pays to keep close tabs on their expense reports, especially during the first few months. You may spot instances in which their fees are inflated, or when they appear to be engaging in unnecessary maintenance activities.

Testing for Environmental Issues

Early in your ownership of a property, pay for tests to see if it has any environmental issues that may require remediation. These tests should address the presence of asbestos, lead-based paint, mold, and radon gas. Asbestos, lead-based paint, and radon gas can cause lung cancer, while mold can irritate the lungs. It requires constant vigilance to minimize mold within a property, so regularly review any potential water leakage areas for mold issues, including windows, skylights, bathrooms, and kitchens. Paying attention to these issues is a form of risk mitigation, since it can prevent tenant lawsuits.

Setting Rental Policies

Immediately after acquiring a property, give some thought to the policies that you want to apply to tenants. All of the following policies will have an impact on how the property will be managed:

- *Lease duration.* If you decide to allow month-to-month lease agreements, then tenants are automatically renewed each month unless they give prior notice. While this approach allows tenants to leave on short notice, it also allows you to change the rent on equally short notice. Since tenants prefer not to move frequently, there tends to be little downside impact to the month-to-month approach. A longer fixed lease term is dominant for commercial and retail properties, and provides the security of multi-year commitments by tenants. The downside of a fixed-term arrangement is that you cannot alter the terms of a lease until it has expired – which may not be for a number of years.
- *Lease rates.* The most essential decision is how much to charge tenants for their use of your property. This is usually based on an analysis of the rates being charged in the area by landlords for similar properties. You can adjust

from this rate based on the age and condition of your property, as well as any differences in the amenities you offer from those offered by the competing properties. It is also useful to compare this rental rate to your costs per month, to see if the property will generate positive cash flow at the indicated rent level.

- *Pets*. Since animals can cause excessive damage and the areas in which they are kept will likely require extensive cleaning at the end of a lease, be sure to state whether pets are allowed and whether an increased deposit will be required in order to keep them on the premises. However, if pets are already kept on the premises, be aware that the imposition of a new no-pets policy will probably drive away their owners, leaving you with empty rental units.
- *Security deposit*. Verify if there are any state-level laws that limit the amount of the security deposit you can charge tenants. This deposit is collected when a tenant moves in and is returned when the party eventually leaves. It is intended to protect you if the tenant damages the property or does not pay the rent. State law may also control what can be deducted from this deposit. Ideally, the deposit amount should be driven by a market analysis, making this a non-factor for prospective tenants comparing required deposits in the area.

Note: State law may mandate that security deposits be held in a separate bank account, where they are held in trust for the tenant. State law may also mandate that interest be paid on the amount deposited, and that tenants be informed of the location of the bank account in which their deposited funds are held.

Ongoing Tenant Relations

Most purchased properties already have tenants on the premises. Whenever there is an ownership change, the tenants will likely have some concerns about what the new owner intends to do. You should address their concerns at once, before they start looking to lease elsewhere. This usually means having a frank discussion about any changes to their rent and facility policies. In addition, be prepared to talk about maintenance issues that have not yet been resolved, including the timing for when you plan to address these items. When discussing these issues, take notes about what you said, so that you can follow up on any promises made. It is essential to follow through on these items, in order to establish your credibility with the people who are providing you with revenue – and especially those whose lease agreements are up for renewal.

Tip: Prepare a letter for each tenant that is distributed as soon as you take ownership, noting the status of their leases, the amount of their security deposits, and all policies, as well as your contact information.

When delivering the just-noted letter to each tenant, schedule a time for a walk-through of their leased space. This is a good time to discuss any additional maintenance issues that they have not yet brought up, as well as to see if the space is being used properly (such as the illegal storage of hazardous materials).

The tenant's existing lease agreements are still in effect, so you will need to wait until they expire before you can impose your own lease agreement on them. This may not take long in the case of month-to-month leases, but may require a lengthy waiting period in cases where leases are still in effect for several more years.

The most critical issue for many investors is how to increase rental rates. One approach is to tie a rate increase to making specific upgrades to a unit, so that the tenant can experience greater value in exchange for the amount paid. Another option is to impose rate increases in increments, perhaps over a number of years, so that tenants will be less inclined to move. In either case, provide the tenants with a table of local rental rates for similar properties, so that they can compare your rates to the rates being charged in the area. Ultimately, the key issue is how to maintain the delicate balance of increasing rates while avoiding the departure of key tenants.

Conducting a Pre-Showing Review

If you show a property with issues to a prospective tenant, that prospect will never turn into an actual tenant. To keep from driving away prospects, be sure to conduct a detailed review of the property first. Here are the most critical issues to investigate:

- That all appliances are working properly, and are visually appealing.
- That all door knobs, latches, windows and doors operate properly.
- That all dowels, hooks, and shelves in the storage areas are working properly.
- That all hazard sensors are operating properly.
- That all kitchen and bathroom surfaces have been thoroughly cleaned.
- That all railings are securely fastened.
- That all windows and screens have been cleaned, and there are no cracks or tears in them.
- That the carpeting and other floor surfaces are clean and undamaged.
- That the circuit breakers are operating properly.
- That the heating, ventilation, and air conditioning system is operating properly.
- That the locks have been changed.
- That the plumbing system delivers both hot and cold water.
- That the wall and ceiling paint provides adequate coverage, without any visible gouges or bare areas.
- That there are no plumbing leaks.

Showing a Property

The easiest way to show a property to prospective tenants is to have a leasing agent or the property manager (if any) do so. If you elect to do so yourself, be aware that you may be asked to return to the property throughout the day to conduct a number of showings. A more efficient approach is to schedule an open house during a time block for which most viewers are likely to be available, such as in the early evening or during the weekend. You can then attend just during these time slots, leaving much more time throughout the day to deal with other issues. An advantage to having multiple prospects touring the property at the same time is that it creates a sense of competition, making it more likely that someone will submit an application.

Rather than leading a tour through a property, it can be more effective to let prospects walk through at their leisure, observe their body language, and listen to their comments. You may be able to use the resulting information to comment on the features of the property that are of most interest to them, thereby increasing their interest in renting space.

> **Tip:** Be sure to give tenants advance warning in writing of your intent to show their rented space to a replacement tenant. This is a common requirement in many states.

A very good reason to maintain your property at a high level is that prospects may ask your current tenants about their rental experience with you – which can have a dramatic effect on your ease of attracting new tenants. Conversely, if you have poor relations with the current tenant, do not show the property until the unit has been vacated, thereby avoiding any uncomfortable conversations.

> **Tip:** If you receive applications from a large number of prospects, this is a possible indicator that you have set the rent too low. Conversely, few applications indicates that a judicious drop in the rate might be in order.

Screening Applicants

An essential ingredient to success in investing is properly screening applicants who want to lease space in your building. Allowing in a bad tenant that does not pay rent, damages the property, and disrupts the neighborhood can wipe out your profits, so take the time to comb through every application. The best way to do so is by mentioning your screening procedure to those parties considering submitting a rental application; once they understand your process, some potential renters may decide not to apply. After that, consider using the following steps in your screening process:

1. Determine the questions to ask. They should cover a person's income, employment, criminal background, credit, and previous eviction and residence history. This investigation should include any co-applicants or co-signers; these parties will also need to complete an application.
2. Verify completion of the rent application. Scan through the document to verify that all required information has been completed and in a legible manner. Also verify that the applicant has signed the form, thereby authorizing you to verify all information provided, and to run a credit report on the person.
3. Verify the applicant's identity. Request to see the person's driver's license, to confirm his or her name and address. If there are discrepancies, inquire as to why, and write down the applicant's responses.
4. Check the applicant's credit. Purchase a credit report, which reveals whether applicants pay their bills on time, as well as any prior bankruptcy filings. Buy

the report from one of the top credit reporting agencies, which are Equifax, Experian, and TransUnion. Dun & Bradstreet can provide reports about commercial applicants.

5. Run a criminal background check. Check both federal and state criminal records to determine if an applicant has a criminal history. It may also be useful to check a sex offender registry and a terrorist watchlist.

6. Verify the applicant's income and employment. If an applicant's gross monthly income is at least three times his or her rent, then they can probably afford to pay the rent. Contact the applicant's current employer to verify the person's employment status, pay rate, and job title, which can give some indication of the person's continued employment. For commercial tenants, ask for a copy of their latest tax return to verify their income.

7. Investigate previous addresses, landlords, and eviction history. The intent is to find out what an applicant paid in rent, whether those payments were made on time, whether the person damaged the property, and whether the landlord had any problems with the party. A good question to ask prior landlords is whether they would rent to the applicant again.

8. Interview the applicant and any co-applicants. After completing the preceding items, conduct an interview. Go over your findings with the applicant, and see if there are any mistakes resulting from your investigation.

9. Accept or reject the applicant. Accept the applicant if the party's gross income is sufficient, he or she has a stable work history, a reasonably high credit score, favorable reviews from prior landlords, and a lack of any felonies or misdemeanors. Be sure to document your findings and resulting decision, in case applicants decide to sue over the issue.

Tip: When screening applicants, be aware of the anti-discrimination provisions of the Fair Housing Act, which prevent you from discriminating against applicants based on a wide variety of factors. To prove that you did not do so, maintain all applications and the associated verification forms and credit reports for at least three years. Also, keep copies of all rejection letters sent to applicants.

Once you select an applicant, do not tell any other applicants about your decision until after the selected party has signed the lease and paid the initial fees. This approach allows you to switch to your second choice if your primary choice drops out.

Tip: Be sure to have the successful applicant sign all rental documents and pay the deposit and first month's rent (preferably with a cashier's check or money order) prior to handing over the keys to the unit. Otherwise, it can be difficult to get the applicant to complete these tasks.

The New Tenant Move-In

An essential element of any move-in is to walk through the unit with the new tenant prior to any items being moved in, and formally document the condition of the property. This information will be needed as a comparison document when the tenant eventually moves out, since you may discover damage to the unit at that point, and want to take a deduction from the security deposit to pay for repairs.

It is especially important to document the condition of the carpeting, since this tends to wear out first, and so could be an item of contention. A tenant should not be charged for ordinary carpet wear, but you may have a valid case if the carpeting has been damaged.

> **Tip:** Consider taking photos of the unit on the move-in date, which can be used as evidence in the event of a dispute with a tenant over damage claims.

Upgrading a Property

One of the best ways to increase the value of a property is to make judicious upgrades that will pay back with increased rents. This involves an ongoing review of your property to see if it is beginning to look dated, and so is in need of an upgrade. In addition, any relatively inexpensive upgrades that improve the looks and/or functionality of the property will probably be worthwhile investments. A good way to decide which upgrades to make is to run a comparison of your property to competing properties in the area, to see if they have certain amenities that your property is lacking.

> **Tip:** Property upgrades are more of a concern when your property is an old one, since it may contain asbestos or lead-based paint. If so, it is generally best to avoid disturbing these materials, since their removal can be extremely expensive.

In residential units, among the more appealing upgrades are granite (or similar) countertops in the bathrooms and kitchen, as well as refinished cabinets in both areas. In addition, ensure that the exterior of the building is attractive, or else prospective tenants will never enter the building. Areas to address may include a parking lot resurfacing, improved landscaping, and updated common areas. Even simple matters, such as a fresh coat of paint, ongoing cleanup activities, and well-trimmed shrubs can make a difference. In particular, ensure that the front entry to the building is always clean and properly painted.

Risk Management Issues

Investment properties tend to be a magnet for lawsuits from tenants. One reason is because some tenants assume the landlord has money (which is not necessarily the case), and so represents an easy source of cash. Another reason is that tenants may spend a large part of their time within the property, which presents a heightened opportunity for issues to arise that can lead to lawsuits. In addition, a landlord may be sued for discrimination after refusing an applicant's request to rent a unit.

There are several ways to deal with these risks. First, enforce a high level of maintenance, and ensure that maintenance issues are dealt with as soon as possible. Doing so minimizes tenant complaints, and also minimizes any risks of injury to them.

Second, remove the clause in your rental agreements that requires the losing party in any lawsuit to pay the legal fees of the prevailing party; this clause is used by tenant rights attorneys to obtain a minor judgment against the landlord, and then pile on substantial attorney fees for reimbursement.

Another risk mitigation option is to schedule ongoing maintenance reviews throughout the property. In addition, respond as soon as possible to all tenant complaints. Document your findings, and verify that all issues found are addressed at once. If possible, have the impacted tenants sign off on a form, stating that the maintenance tasks were completed; this provides evidence that the tenants are satisfied with the changes you have made.

Yet another mitigation possibility is to verify that your suppliers all have insurance coverage, and that the legal entity owning your property is named on the suppliers' policies as an additional insured. Evidence of this coverage should be provided before you allow a supplier to conduct any work on the property. In addition, maintain a file of these additional insured documents, and review it regularly to ensure that all coverage is still current.

Consider bringing in a risk management expert (perhaps recommended by your insurer), who will review your property and point out any risks that can be eliminated or at least mitigated. For example, you might install an alarm on any doors leading to the roof, so that you will be warned when anyone is up there.

Insurance Coverage

It is impossible to eliminate all risks from a property, so you will need to acquire insurance coverage, thereby offloading the residual risk to an insurer. This does not mean that you must acquire all possible types of insurance, since risks are only likely to materialize in a few specific areas.

A liability policy will be needed that provides protection against lawsuits, while also paying for the legal fees required to defend against these suits. This policy will protect against losses or personal injuries suffered by anyone as the result of defective or dangerous conditions within the property.

When shopping for rental property insurance, you will find that there are different types of policies, which are called forms. These forms have different levels of coverage. The following descriptions generally state the nature of these forms:

- *DP-1*. Rental property insurance is categorized as a dwelling policy, or DP, and the DP-1 is the cheapest form with the most basic coverage. DP-1 forms usually only cover named perils, meaning that if a peril or disaster is not explicitly named in the form, you will not be reimbursed for the damage. These policies often provide reimbursements on an actual cash value basis, meaning that the insurer will pay you for covered damage minus wear and tear.
- *DP-2*. This form provides slightly broader coverage than the DP-1. Like the DP-1, its coverage tends to be on a named peril basis. However, DP-2 coverage will generally extend to a broader range of perils. For example, an insurer might offer coverage for burglary damage in its DP-2 policy but not in its DP-1. The DP-2 form also improves on the DP-1 by typically providing

coverage on a replacement cost basis, meaning that damage will be covered at the price it would take to cover the damage at current market prices.

- *DP-3*. This form, which is the most expensive option, provides the broadest range of coverage of the three forms. It provides extensive peril coverage, protecting against all perils except those explicitly excluded in the policy. Like the DP-2 policy, its coverage will be provided on a replacement cost basis.

An insurance policy costs more when your property is older and not in the best shape. In some cases, it may not be possible to obtain insurance at all, especially in areas where insurers have experienced significant payouts in the past. It can be useful to make inquiries with your insurer to see if anything can be installed (such as a fire sprinkler system) that will reduce the policy cost.

Tip: If you are renting space in your home, have your insurance agent convert your homeowner's policy into a landlord's policy; this policy provides special coverage that is not present in a homeowner's policy.

There may be a *coinsurance* provision in an insurance policy. This provision is designed to penalize the insured party if it under-insures the value of property. Coinsurance is stated as a percentage. The following example illustrates the concept.

EXAMPLE

Fred owns a commercial building, which has a replacement cost of $3,000,000. The company's property insurance contains an 80% coinsurance clause, which means that the insured amount must be at least 80% of the replacement cost of the building, or $2,400,000. The actual amount insured is for $2,000,000. Since the insured value is less than 80% of its replacement value, a loss payout under the policy will be subjected to an under-reporting penalty.

The building subsequently suffers $500,000 of property damage. The amount paid to Fred by the insurer is calculated as follows:

$2,000,000 insured amount ÷ (80% coinsurance percentage × $3,000,000 replacement cost) × $500,000 loss

= $416,667

In essence, Fred pays an $83,333 penalty because he did not insure the full value of the property.

The most commonly-used coinsurance percentage is 80%. If the percentage is higher, the insurer is imposing a stricter standard on the insured entity to insure the full value of property.

Given the negative impact of the coinsurance provision, you must routinely examine the values of your insured property to verify that adequate amounts of insurance are being carried. Otherwise, a loss could result in a significantly reduced payout by the insurer.

Tip: If you own multiple properties, you may be able to obtain better coverage by purchasing a single policy that covers all of the properties.

Umbrella coverage is a separate policy that provides an extra tranche of coverage for a general liability policy. It is not activated unless a loss exceeds the per occurrence or aggregate limits on the underlying liability policy. The underlying coverage must be maintained for the umbrella coverage to take effect. Umbrella coverage is especially useful when you own a larger property.

There are several other insurance possibilities worth considering. One is loss-of-rents insurance, where (as the name implies) you are reimbursed for any rents lost if your property sustains heavy damage. Also, consider obtaining non-owned auto liability coverage, which provides liability protection if your employees cause accidents or injuries while operating their own vehicles. Another option is flood or earthquake coverage, which pays for damage caused by these events (though it is usually very expensive, with a high deductible). Finally, consider obtaining a fidelity bond, which provides reimbursement when a dishonest employee steals money from your business (usually rent payments).

A *deductible* is the initial loss amount that must be absorbed by the insured party. If you elect to absorb a large deductible, then the insurer will reduce the price of the insurance offered. If you have significant cash reserves, it can make sense to accept a higher deductible, thereby saving money on insurance premiums that can be put to other uses.

Insurance claims can be substantial, so be sure to organize your insurance management system to ensure that insurance policies are current and claims are properly made. This means maintaining a policy tracking system to know when each policy expires, so that you can renew them on a timely basis. Also, fully document all insurable issues as soon as they arise, and photograph or make videos of the damaged areas. In addition, contact your insurance agent as soon as possible about making a claim, and also document your claims. Keep a copy of all claims on file, to provide backup in case a litigant makes a claim against you years later. Paying attention to these issues will maximize your use of insurance policies.

Creating a Filing System

There is a substantial amount of paperwork associated with owning a property. It may be tempting to throw all of your property-related paperwork into a box and only dredge up items when absolutely necessary, but a better approach is to introduce a high degree of organization to your record keeping. The following best practices are advised:

- Maintain separate records for each property. This might involve the use of a separate accordion filing box for each one, or allocating a separate drawer in a filing cabinet to each one.

    o For each property, maintain a separate ownership file. This should include your final purchase offer, contract, closing statement, appraisal, insurance policies, due diligence inspection, environmental reports, loan documents, and any associated correspondence. In addition, put your deed in a bank safety-deposit box, and keep a copy of it on file.

    o For each property, maintain a separate folder for each category of expense, such as maintenance and utilities. These folders should be archived at the end of the year and replaced with new ones.

    o For each property, maintain a separate maintenance file. This should include the expenditures for all maintenance and capital improvements made during your ownership of the property. This information is useful for calculating your basis in the property, which is needed when it is eventually sold.

        ▪ For each unit within a property, maintain a separate tenant file that includes the party's rental application, lease agreement, maintenance requests, charges and payments, along with any correspondence. These files are archived and replaced with new ones whenever a tenant moves out.

        ▪ For each unit within a property, maintain a separate maintenance file. This file should contain the records pertaining to all maintenance issues and capital improvements made, along with the related receipts. Be sure to keep track of the installation dates for all appliances and other equipment installed in a unit. Keep this file open even when tenants depart and are replaced by new ones.

Consider storing all records in a fireproof safe, including archived records. Doing so can prevent catastrophic paperwork losses in the event of a fire.

For more information about the accounting for real estate, see the author's *Real Estate Accounting* book.

Summary

It takes a significant amount of ongoing management to ensure that the cash flows from an investment property are maximized. This is not easy when you own several properties, or when a property is located far away from where you live. Consequently, it is generally best to hire a high-quality property management company to oversee your property. When this is done, you will not be directly involved in the screening of applicants, but you will still be responsible for ensuring that all necessary insurance is current. Though being prudent is always important when running a property, you should not scrimp on your insurance coverage – doing so could result in significant losses.

Chapter 8
Tax Considerations

Introduction

The tax laws in the United States are generally structured to favor those who invest in real estate. Having a solid understanding of the applicable tax laws can significantly improve your return from real estate investments. In this chapter, we cover the tax impact of property acquisitions and dispositions, depreciation, and several related matters.

When reviewing the tax considerations in this chapter, keep in mind that they are based on current tax law – which could change at any time. Given the inherently short-term nature of any tax law, you should not acquire a property just based on the tax benefits of doing so. Instead, the primary consideration is whether the acquisition makes economic sense, after which you should consider the tax consequences.

Tax Impact of Property Acquisitions

There is hardly any immediate tax consequence associated with the initial acquisition of real estate. However, the manner in which this acquisition is conducted can have numerous ramifications later on. In the following sub-sections, we note the most essential aspects of a real estate acquisition from a tax perspective.

Acquisition Costs

Some costs associated with an acquisition are included in the cost of the property, and so have no immediate tax effect. Other acquisition expenses are considered to be current expenses, and so can be used as tax deductions in the current period. It can be difficult to differentiate between these two types of expenses, especially when a property has been constructed, and the expense types have been intermingled.

Basis

Basis is the amount of capital investment in a property for tax purposes. In most cases, basis is the cost of real estate to the owner, which is the amount paid for it in cash, debt obligations, and other property or services. The cost of real estate includes sales taxes and other expenses connected with the purchase. The basis in one's property is a critical issue, because it is used to determine the amount of any gain or loss when the property is eventually dispositioned.

EXAMPLE

An investor owns a small office building that has an adjusted basis of $1,500,000. If the building is sold for its current market value of $1,800,000, the investor must report a gain of $300,000; this is the difference between the amount realized on the sale and the basis of the property.

Original Basis

We referred to adjusted basis in the preceding example. *Adjusted basis* is the original basis of a property, with adjustments for events occurring through the disposition date. There are several ways to determine the original basis of property, depending on how it was acquired. The various approaches are as follows:

- *Property is purchased.* When property is purchased, then the owner's original basis is its cost. Cost is the amount of cash paid to the seller, as well as the amount of any associated mortgage, and any acquisition expenses, such as legal fees, title insurance premiums, and commissions.
- *Property is acquired by gift.* When a property is acquired by gift, its original basis is the basis the donor had in the property, adjusted for any gift tax paid at the time of the transfer.
- *Property is acquired by option.* When the holder of an option exercises it in order to acquire a property, the cost of the option is added to the price paid for the property in order to arrive at its original basis.
- *Property is acquired from a spouse.* A transfer of property from one spouse to the other (or to a former spouse as part of a divorce) is treated as a gift, so the original basis for the donee is the basis the donor had in the property.
- *Property is acquired in an exchange.* When a property held for use in a trade or business or for investment is exchanged for a similar property, the basis of the old property becomes the basis of the new property that was acquired in exchange for the old one. This is considered a substitute basis, since the basis of the old property is substituted for the new one.
- *Property is constructed by owner.* When the owner constructs a property, then the owner's original basis is the cost of materials and contractor fees, as well as the property's share of other costs that are allocable to the property during its construction phase. This allocated cost rule applies to business property, but not to a personal residence.
- *Property is inherited.* When a property is inherited, its original basis is set at the fair market value of the property on the day when the decedent dies.

As just noted, the original basis of a property includes the amount of any associated mortgage. The basis also includes the amount of any existing mortgage on the property that the buyer is taking on as part of the purchase transaction.

EXAMPLE

Sally Emerson buys real estate for $350,000. This payment is comprised of $100,000 in cash, a $110,000 mortgage, and her assumption of an existing mortgage on the property of $140,000. Her original cost basis in the property is $350,000.

Note: Borrowing against property that you already own does not impact its basis.

When it appears that a taxpayer is purchasing property with an inflated amount of debt in order to inflate the associated basis in the property, the basis is limited to the property's fair market value.

EXAMPLE

David Morris buys real estate with a $500,000 down payment and a mortgage with a principal amount of $4,500,000. The fair market value of the property at the time of the purchase is $4,000,000. The basis of the property for tax purposes is $4,000,000, which reflects its fair value, rather than the inflated $5,000,000 value implied by the excessively large mortgage.

We noted earlier that the original basis of a property will include a number of extra expenses that are associated with the purchase transaction. The general rule is that all expenses related to the acquisition of property are part of its original basis. Examples of acquisition costs that must be recorded in this manner are noted in the following exhibit.

Examples of Acquisition Costs

Appraisal fees	Condemnation costs	Title abstract
Attorney's fees	Credit investigations	Title defense
Clearing and grading	Improvements to property	Title insurance
Closing costs	Mortgage title insurance	Title determination
Commissions	Survey costs	Utility connection costs

Any amounts paid to facilitate the acquisition or production of property must be capitalized. This activity occurs when the payment is made in the process of investigating an acquisition. The facilitative acquisition costs noted in the following bullet points should be included in the original basis of a property:

- Calculating application fees and similar costs
- Evaluating the property title
- Negotiating the terms of a deal
- Obtaining an appraisal
- Obtaining consulting services related to the property

- Obtaining permits linked to the acquisition
- Obtaining tax advice for a property deal
- Payment of broker commissions
- Payment of sales taxes and transfer taxes
- Payment of title registration fees
- Preparing and reviewing the purchase agreement

EXAMPLE

A purveyor of surfing equipment currently operates a string of retail establishments down the coast of California, and is interested in opening stores in Hawaii. As the first step in doing so, the firm hires a development consulting firm to examine this new market to conduct surveys and examine zoning requirements, ultimately suggesting where to place stores. In addition, the firm hires an appraiser to develop appraisals for three prospective sites in Hawaii, with the intent of using this information to decide whether to make offers on these properties. Once this preliminary work is complete, the firm decides to make offers on two of the three sites.

Of these expenditures, the fees charged by the development consulting firm are not capitalized, because they are not inherently facilitative costs. However, the firm should certainly capitalize all payments made to the appraiser, since these are inherently facilitative costs. This means that the appraisal costs allocable to the acquired properties should be added to their original basis. However, the appraisal costs associated with the property that was not acquired can be classified as a deductible expense.

> **Note:** Once a buyer takes title to a property, all costs related to installation, repairs and testing should be capitalized until the property is placed in service.

EXAMPLE

Alfred Mundy buys a run-down and unoccupied medical office building for $3 million, and spends an additional $200,000 over the next few months to fix up a variety of problems around the property, including concrete repairs, curb replacements, plumbing overhauls, and repairs to the air conditioning system. Following this work, Mr. Mundy starts renting out the facility to doctors. The $200,000 repair cost should be capitalized into the original basis of the property.

When the total original cost of a property acquisition has been decided upon, this figure may need to be allocated among several different elements of a real estate acquisition, particularly between depreciable improvements and non-depreciable land. This process results in a separate original basis for each asset.

> **Note:** A separate cost allocation is not necessary when a personal residence is acquired, since it is not held for business or investment use. There is no depreciation of a personal residence, so there is no need for an allocation between a land asset and other assets.

The allocation of costs between the elements of a real estate acquisition is normally derived from the relative fair market values of the underlying assets.

EXAMPLE

Sarah Dempsey buys a warehouse and the land on which it sits for $600,000, and also incurs $40,000 of expenses that are related to the transaction. This means that her original basis in the property is $640,000. Based on the fair market value of the land and the fair market value of the warehouse, the land's value is 30% of the total value, while the warehouse's value is 70%. Thus, the basis for the land is $192,000 and the basis for the warehouse is $448,000.

As a substitute for fair market value when allocating costs, it may be acceptable to use the valuations derived for property tax assessments, appraisals by appraisal professionals, and replacement cost.

There is no allocation for building demolition costs between land and other elements of a real estate acquisition. Instead, the full cost of the demolition is included in the cost basis for the land. If there was any remaining basis in the building that was demolished, this basis is carried over to the basis of the land on which the building was situated.

> **Tip:** Land improvements may be depreciable. When this is the case, as much of a cost allocation as possible should be directed away from the land asset and towards the land improvements asset. For example, the general cost of grading land is fully allocated to the land, while grading prior to paving a road is allocated to the road asset.

The period over which the cost of personal property can be depreciated is shorter than for real property, so one may consider allocating some portion of the cost of a property acquisition to personal property, when such an allocation can be justified. Property associated with real estate that may be considered personal property include such items as carpeting, removable floor coverings, removable partitions, pictures, and special lighting. Generally, items that are designed to be removable, and which are removable without harming a building, and which can still be used after their removal, can be considered personal property.

A further allocation will be needed when real estate is bought along with a working business. In this case, the amount of the purchase price allocated to tangible and then intangible assets is capped at their fair market value, with the remaining amount paid being allocated to goodwill.

EXAMPLE

Fred McMurtry buys a small business for $300,000. The purchase includes real estate with a fair market value of $180,000 and intangible assets with a fair market value of $30,000. Therefore, he assigns $180,000 of the cost to real estate, $30,000 to personal property, and $90,000 to goodwill.

Costs Relating to Constructed Assets

The costs to construct a property are capitalized, and so form the original basis for it. The costs that must be capitalized include the following:

- All direct construction costs, such as materials and labor
- All costs of direct labor, including compensation, overtime, payroll taxes, and benefits
- All costs of indirect labor, such as supervisory and clerical positions
- All materials consumed in the course of constructing the property
- All quality control and inspection materials and labor
- Bidding, engineering, and design expenses related to the project
- Depreciation on the equipment and facilities used to construct the property
- Interest on the funds borrowed to finance the project for the project duration[7]
- Repairs and maintenance conducted on the equipment used to construct the property
- Utilities related to the project
- Insurance on the equipment and facilities used during the project
- Rental costs for all equipment and facilities related to the property
- Tools consumed during the project

Cost areas related to a construction project that should *not* be capitalized include marketing, selling, theft losses, income taxes, and depreciation on idle equipment.

Real Estate Financing Issues

Many real estate acquisitions are financed in large part with debt, where the underlying property is used as collateral on the debt. In the following sub-sections, we cover a number of issues pertaining to the debt associated with real estate financing.

---

[7] The amount of interest to capitalize is that amount of interest that would have been avoided if the construction project had not taken place.

Mortgage Financing

The following points clarify the tax impact of obtaining mortgage financing for a property:

- *Mortgage costs.* When a borrower obtains a mortgage, the attendant mortgage costs (such as fees and commissions) are amortized over the term of the mortgage. Amortization is calculated on a straight-line basis. Thus, if an investor obtains a mortgage to finance the acquisition of business property and the mortgage term is 10 years, then the associated $4,000 of mortgage costs must be deducted over 10 years, at $400 per year. If an investor pays off a loan, then any remaining unamortized mortgage costs should be deducted at that time. The same accelerated deduction approach applies when a property is sold off; any remaining unamortized costs are deducted as of the sale date.
- *Payment discounts.* When the remaining balance on a mortgage obligation is forgiven, the borrower recognizes income on the amount forgiven.
- *Prepayment penalty.* When an investor pays a lender a prepayment penalty in order to pay off a mortgage early, the penalty is treated as additional interest expense.
- *Refinancing.* When a mortgage is refinanced, it may be for a larger amount than the previous mortgage iteration. If so, there is no immediate tax impact. Instead, it constitutes a tax-free source of cash for the investor.
- *Subsidized mortgages.* A construction company may offer to subsidize a portion of a buyer's mortgage payments in order to close a deal. These subsidization payments are treated as an ordinary expense of the seller, or as a reduction of the sale price – the tax effect is the same either way.

Interest Issues

With a number of limitations, the interest paid or accrued on mortgage debt is deductible in the year incurred. A cash-basis[8] taxpayer deducts the amount of interest actually paid, while an accrual-basis taxpayer deducts interest as it accrues over the term of the mortgage. The key limitations on this rule are as follows:

- *Capitalized interest.* Interest is capitalized when it is incurred during the construction of real estate.
- *At-risk rule.* Interest can only be deducted up to the amount of an owner's investment that is at risk (as discussed later in the At-Risk Rules section).
- *Prepaid interest.* When a taxpayer makes a prepaid interest payment, it can only be deducted ratably over the term of the mortgage (not upfront). Points may be considered prepaid interest if they are not paid in exchange for lender services.

---

[8] Cash basis accounting involves recording revenue when cash is received, and expenses when cash is paid. Accrual basis accounting involves recording revenue when earned, and expenses when consumed.

- *Business interest.* The amount of deductible business interest for any form of business entity is capped at 30% of the taxpayer's adjusted taxable income, with any disallowed amounts being carried forward indefinitely. Business interest is the interest on debt allocable to a business, and does not include investment interest. This rule does not apply to a small business using the cash basis of accounting. A taxpayer can elect to exclude from this limitation the interest associated with a real property business[9].
- *Imputed interest.* The seller of real estate may provide financing to the buyer as part of the sale of a property. When the interest rate associated with this financing is too low or nonexistent, the taxpayer is required to impute an interest rate based on a statutory minimum interest rate (which is based on the interest rate on certain United States government debt). Doing so reduces the principal part of the seller financing by shifting a portion of the payments due over to interest expense.

Passive Activity Losses

There are rules regarding the extent to which gains can be offset with losses. Under the passive activity loss rules, losses and tax credits derived from passive activities can only be applied against income from passive activities. If these rules result in a loss or tax credit not being used, then it can be carried forward into future years and applied to passive income in those periods. Any passive activity loss that is still unused when a taxpayer disposes of the related passive activity can deduct it as a non-passive activity loss as of the disposal date. The rules apply when an activity involves a business in which the taxpayer has no material participation. Rental activities are considered to be passive (irrespective of a taxpayer's level of activity in it), as is owning a limited partnership interest.

Clearly, the concept of material participation is key to determining whether one is subject to the passive activity rules. Material participation in a business can be proven if a person's actions meet any one of the following tests:

- The person participates in the business more than 500 hours per year.
- The person's participation comprises essentially all of the participation in the business by anyone.
- The person participates in the business more than 100 hours per year, and this participation is no less than the participation of any other party.
- The person has materially participated in the business for any five of the last 10 years.
- The person provided personal services at a material level for any three years prior to the current year.
- The person participates in the business on a regular, continuous, and substantial basis during the year.

---

[9] A real property trade or business includes a real estate development, construction, acquisition, conversion, rental, operation, management, leasing, or brokerage business.

The other key point in the passive activity rules is that rental activities are considered to be passive. Therefore, what constitutes a rental activity? Such an activity is present when property is used by customers, and the income generated from this activity is for the use of the property. To avoid a designation as a rental activity, a property must meet one of the following criteria:

- The average period of property use by customers is seven days or fewer.
- The average period of property use by customers is 30 days or fewer, and significant personal services are provided by the owner or someone on behalf of the owner.
- The owner or someone working on the owner's behalf provides extraordinary personal services, not matter how long customers use the property.
- The property rental is incidental to some other nonrental activity; this is the case when gross rental income is less than two percent of the lesser of the fair market value of the property or its unadjusted basis.
- The property is made available during business hours for the nonexclusive use of customers.

EXAMPLE

A taxpayer owns and operates a business-oriented longer-term residency facility. It is mostly used by executives who need to reside in the area for a period of time, usually about two weeks. The taxpayer provides basic cleaning services to customers, along with a twice-a-week linen service and daily room cleaning. The cost of the services provided to customers by the taxpayer is approximately eight percent of the occupancy fees charged to customers. Given these facts, the taxpayer is not providing significant personal services to customers. Consequently, the taxpayer is engaged in a rental activity, and so is subject to the passive activity loss rules.

EXAMPLE

A taxpayer owns 300 acres of unimproved land with a fair market value of $100,000 and an unadjusted basis of $85,000. The taxpayer intends to continue holding the land in expectation that it will appreciate in value over time. To minimize the cost of holding the land, the taxpayer leases a portion of the land to an organic farmer in exchange for $1,600 per year. Since the gross rental income from the land is less than two percent of the adjusted basis of the land, the rental activity is considered incidental to the main purpose of the taxpayer, which is to hold it for investment purposes. Therefore, the taxpayer is not subject to the passive activity loss rules.

There is a real property business exception to the passive activity loss rules. A *real property business* is any operation that engages in the development, construction, acquisition, conversion, rental, operation, management, brokerage or leasing of real estate. Under this exception, the real estate activities of a qualifying party are not passive if the party participates at a material level in the activity. To qualify for the exception, a person must perform more than half of the personal services performed during the year in real property businesses, and spend more than 750 hours of services during that time in real property activities. Some form of documentation must be kept to prove that the requisite time was indeed spent on the indicated activities.

At-Risk Rules

The tax regulations cap the amount of losses that a real estate investor can recognize, which are known as the at-risk rules. The intent behind the at-risk rules is to prevent the use of tax shelters that use various techniques to give investors more deductions than they invest in a property. In essence, the deductions that an investor can recognize are limited to the sum of the following:

- Any amounts borrowed for which the investor has posted property as collateral, up to the fair market value of the party's interest in the collateralized property;
- Any amounts borrowed for which the investor is personally liable;
- Qualified non-recourse financing for the property;
- The adjusted basis of any other property contributed to the activity; and
- The amount of money actually invested in the property.

EXAMPLE

An investor puts $40,000 into a business property and also obtains a $120,000 recourse loan to finance it. Since the investor is personally liable for the loan, the entire $160,000 investment is at risk. During the first year of operations, $5,000 of the loan is paid off and the property generates $10,000 of income. There is no distribution to the investor. This means that the amount at risk at year-end is $165,000, which is calculated as the $160,000 initial amount at risk, minus the $5,000 loan payoff, plus the $10,000 of income generated.

The deductions generated by a property can always be recognized, as long as there is a sufficient amount of offsetting income also being generated by that property. Beyond that point, additional deductions can be taken to the extent that an investor is at risk, as outlined in the previous bullet points.

EXAMPLE

An investor invests $100,000 in a business property by investing $25,000 in cash and obtaining a non-recourse loan for the remaining $75,000. Given the structure of this financing, the investor is only at risk for $25,000. At the end of the year, the property has generated $30,000 of deductions for the investor. Of this amount, the investor can only deduct $25,000, which is the amount at risk. The $5,000 balance of the loss cannot be deducted, but can be rolled forward to be offset against either any future income generated by the property, or any other amount at risk that the investor elects to invest in the property.

If an amount formerly at risk in a property is no longer at risk and a loss deduction had been allowed against it, then this deduction must be recaptured.

EXAMPLE

An investor puts $30,000 of cash and a $70,000 recourse loan into a property investment, so that all $100,000 of the investment is at risk. The investor then takes $40,000 in loss deductions, after which the loan is converted to a non-recourse loan. Since the investor is no longer at risk for the loan, only $30,000 of his investment is at risk. This means that the investor must report $10,000 of income that represents the recapture of the loss deductions in excess of the $30,000 cash investment.

Depreciation

Much of the cost of a property can be recaptured through depreciation, which is the ratable deduction of tangible asset costs over a period of time, reflecting the rate at which they wear out. The following sub-sections describe depreciation conventions and Section 179 deductions.

Depreciation Conventions

The following points relate to the use of depreciation:

- *Depreciation usage.* A depreciation deduction is only allowed for property used for business, or which is held for the production of income. Depreciation is not allowed on any property held for personal use. Also, depreciation can only be taken on property that is subject to wear and tear, which means that land cannot be depreciated.
- *Start date.* Depreciation begins when a property is placed in service.
- *MACRS.* Depreciation is calculated using the Modified Accelerated Cost Recovery System, which puts assets into classes that have set depreciation periods.
- *Basis of calculation.* Depreciation is calculated using the tax basis of a property.
- *Depreciation period.* The period over which depreciation is calculated depends on the class to which a property is assigned; the various classifications are noted in the following table. These classes provide for depreciation periods that may be anywhere from three to 50 years. Residential rental property has a depreciation period of 27.5 years, while nonresidential property has a period of 39 years.
- *Calculation convention.* The straight-line depreciation method is to be used for residential rental and nonresidential real property. In addition, the *mid-month convention* is applied to residential rental and nonresidential real property. Under this convention, one-half of the normal depreciation rate is applied to the first and last months to be depreciated.

- *In-service date.* A constructed building is considered to have been placed in service (and is therefore depreciable) when a significant portion of it has been finished and made available for use. A good indicator of this is when a certificate of occupancy has been issued for it. This can result in depreciation commencing for different floors of a multi-floor office building at different times, depending on when they are completed.
- *Additions and improvements.* Any additions to and improvements of property are recorded and depreciated as separate property items. The depreciation calculation assumptions for each of these items is the same as the assumptions used for the underlying property. For example, the cost of an improvement to residential rental property would also be depreciated over 27.5 years, using straight-line depreciation and the mid-month convention.

Tip: Given the extremely long depreciation periods for additions and improvements, it makes sense to classify as much ongoing property work as possible as repairs, so that they can be deducted at once.

MACRS Classes and Depreciation Periods (relevant items are noted in bold)

Class	Depreciation Period	Description
3-year property	3 years	Tractor units for over-the-road use, race horses over 2 years old when placed in service, any other horse over 12 years old when placed in service, **qualified rent-to-own property**
5-year property	5 years	Automobiles, taxis, buses, trucks, computers and peripheral equipment, office equipment, any property used in research and experimentation, breeding cattle and dairy cattle, **appliances and etc. used in residential rental real estate activity**, certain green energy property
7-year property	7 years	Office furniture and fixtures, agricultural machinery and equipment, any property not designated as being in another class, natural gas gathering lines
10-year property	10 years	Vessels, barges, tugs, **single-purpose agricultural or horticultural structures**, trees/vines bearing fruits or nuts, qualified small electric meter and smart electric grid systems
15-year property	15 years	**Certain land improvements** (such as shrubbery, fences, roads, sidewalks and bridges), retail motor fuel outlets, municipal wastewater treatment plants, clearing and grading land improvements for gas utility property, electric transmission property, natural gas distribution lines
20-year property	20 years	**Farm buildings** (other than those noted under 10-year property), municipal sewers not categorized as 25-year property, the initial clearing and grading of land for electric utility transmission and distribution plants
25-year property	25 years	Property that is an integral part of the water distribution facilities, municipal sewers

Class	Depreciation Period	Description
Residential rental property	27.5 years	**Any building or structure where 80% or more of its gross rental income is from dwelling units**
Nonresidential real property	39 years	**An office building, store, or warehouse that is not residential property or has a class life of less than 27.5 years**

Land improvements were noted in the preceding table as being 15-year property. These investments do not permanently improve the land; instead, they improve it only for use with a specific building. Thus, digging prior to the construction of a building would be classified as a land improvement expenditure, while general grading of the land is included in the cost basis of the land. Also, expenditures for general landscaping are included in the cost basis of the land. Land improvement expenditures are to be depreciated over 15 years, using the 150% declining balance method and the half-year convention.

Section 179

IRS Code Section 179 allows business owners to take an immediate tax deduction for the cost of tangible depreciable personal property, rather than depreciating these assets over an extended period of time. By doing so, one can defer the payment of income taxes until a later period. The types of fixed assets to which the Section 179 deduction applies include business machinery and equipment, computers, office equipment, livestock and vehicles. While these items cannot be considered real estate, some qualified real property is eligible for Section 179 treatment, including nonresidential improvements to roofs, security systems, fire protection and alarm systems, and heating, ventilation, and air-conditioning property. The deduction can be taken in the year in which an asset is put into service. There is a cap on the amount of Section 179 deductions in each year, which is inflation adjusted.

Tax Impact of Real Estate Disposition

The manner in which a property owner disposes of real estate can have a profound impact on the resulting tax consequences. In this section, we address a number of issues relating to the disposal of property, including depreciation recapture, property exchanges, installment sales, and the demolition of property.

Sale of Real Estate

The calculation of any gain or loss associated with the sale of real estate is the difference between the adjusted basis of the property and the amount realized from its sale. The amount realized from a property sale is the total of all cash received, plus the fair market value of any property or services received, plus the remaining balance on any associated liabilities that are being assumed by the buyer. The amount realized is reduced by any selling costs, which include broker commissions, state and local taxes, and mortgage recording taxes.

A gain arises when the amount realized from a sale is greater than a property's adjusted basis, while a loss arises in the reverse situation.

EXAMPLE

Ms. Jones buys a small office building for $1 million, makes $200,000 of improvements to it, and claims $40,000 in depreciation deductions. Her adjusted basis in the property is therefore $1,160,000. She then sells the building for $800,000 in cash and property with a fair market value of $500,000. As part of the sale transaction, the buyer takes on an existing $200,000 mortgage. $35,000 of selling expenses are incurred as part of the deal. Ms. Jones must recognize a gain of $305,000, which is calculated as the total of the cash and property received, as well as the assumption of the existing mortgage (totaling $1,465,000), minus the adjusted basis of $1,160,000.

Characterization of Gains and Losses

Once a gain or loss associated with the sale of property has been determined, it must be characterized as either capital or ordinary. Most personal and investment assets are considered by default to be capital assets, from which capital gains and losses are derived. Those assets considered to be noncapital in nature (and from which ordinary gains and losses are derived) include the following general types:

- Inventory assets
- Depreciable property used in a business
- Real property used in a business
- Accounts and notes receivable obtained in the ordinary course of business
- Copyrights, literary creations, artistic compositions, and similar assets
- Supplies consumed in the ordinary course of business

When a capital gain occurs, it must be classified as either a short-term gain or a long-term one (where the associated property was held for more than one year). This classification is needed to deal with the differing tax rates that apply to each type of gain.

Depreciable property used in a business and real property used in a business are provided special tax treatment under IRC Section 1231. In essence, all gains and losses related to these assets within a year are combined, with any aggregate net gains treated as capital gains and any aggregate net losses treated as ordinary losses. The following assets are an example of the types of assets that are covered by Section 1231:

- Depreciable personal property used in a business and held for more than one year
- Real property (such as income-producing real estate) used in a business and held for more than one year
- Property held for the production of rents or royalties and held for more than one year
- Leaseholds used in a business and held for more than one year

> **Tip:** To take full advantage of Section 1231, time the disposition of various properties so that all gains are recognized in the year prior to all losses. Doing so maximizes the amount of capital gains that can be recognized. Recognizing gains in the years following the recognition of losses triggers a recapture rule that converts the gains into ordinary income.

Depreciation Recapture

A depreciation deduction is used during the holding period for property in order to establish a noncash expense that offsets the amount of income generated by the property; the result is a *decline* in ordinary income. The downside of depreciation is that these deductions also reduce the basis in property, thereby *increasing* the amount of gain recognized when that property is eventually sold; the result is an increased capital gain.

There are two cases in which depreciation must be recaptured for the purpose of calculating the gain or loss on property. Section 1245 states that all prior depreciation and amortization deductions be recaptured as ordinary income to the extent of any gain realized when a property is sold. There are several types of property subject to Section 1245, of which the most relevant are personal property and certain types of tangible depreciable property.

Section 1250 describes the other situation in which depreciation must be recaptured. Section 1250 states that all prior depreciation and amortization deductions be recaptured as ordinary income to the extent that excess depreciation was taken. Excess depreciation is any depreciation deduction taken that exceeds the amount calculated using the straight-line depreciation method. If property is held for less than one year, then all depreciation taken is characterized as excess depreciation. In short, Section 1250 is triggered when depreciation was calculated using any accelerated depreciation method, and does not apply when the straight-line method was used. The types of property covered by Section 1250 include residential real property, any real property depreciated using the straight-line method, low-income housing, and real property located outside the country.

Property Exchanges

We covered property exchanges in Chapter 1 of this book.

Installment Sales

We covered installment sales in Chapter 1 of this book.

Home Use for Rental

It is quite common for a person to rent out a portion of his or her home. When this is done, the rent received is treated as taxable income. However, someone who rents property for less than 15 days during the year and uses it as a personal residence the rest of the time does not have to include the rent in his or her income; when this is done, the person is prohibited from deducting any rental expenses.

The compilation of rent-related expenses is somewhat more complicated, since it involves dividing expenditures between those parts of the home that are used for rental activities and those for personal activities. The method used should be the same approach just described for a home being used for a business. An additional allocation method that may be appropriate when providing meals to tenants is to divide food costs by the number of people in the house.

Home Converted to Investment Property

A taxpayer may convert his or her residence into a rental property. If so, the taxpayer can treat it as an investment property, allowing for the use of the various deductions described earlier for a business or investment property. When this is done, the taxpayer can depreciate it as of the conversion date based on the lower of its fair market value or the adjusted basis of the property.

Tax Management Strategies

The typical taxpayer wants to defer the payment of taxes to a later period, in order to have use of the funds that would otherwise be used to pay taxes. To do so, the best tax management strategy is to defer the recognition of income and accelerate the recognition of deductions. Less commonly, a taxpayer might seek to pay taxes sooner, usually because tax rates are expected to increase in the future. In the latter case, the best strategy is to accelerate the recognition of income and defer the recognition of deductions. In the following sub-sections, we address the tax management strategies that can be applied to each situation.

Tax Deferral Strategy

The following strategies are sub-divided into those applicable to cash-basis taxpayers and accrual-basis taxpayers.

Cash-Basis Tax Deferral Strategies

- Delay billings related to properties until after year-end.
- Delay collection activities on billings until after year-end.
- Keep repair work separate from renovation work, so that the repairs can be deducted.
- Pay for advance purchases of supplies and maintenance.
- Pay for depreciable personal property in the current year to create a deduction.
- Pay out bonuses in the current year.
- Prepay real estate taxes in the current year.
- Sell property in the current year on which there will be a loss.
- Set a closing date after year-end to sell a property on which there will be a gain.

<u>Accrual-Basis Tax Deferral Strategies</u>

- Buy depreciable personal property in the current year to create a deduction.
- Accelerate the completion of service contracts into the current year.
- Accelerate the furnishing of property into the current year.
- Keep repair work separate from renovation work, so that the repairs can be deducted.
- Make advance purchases of supplies and maintenance, to be received in the current year.
- Sell property in the current year for which there will be a loss.
- Set a closing date after year-end to sell property on which there will be a gain.
- Recognize the obligation for bonus payouts in the current year.

Tax Acceleration Strategy

In order to accelerate the recognition of taxable income, cash-basis and accrual-basis taxpayers should follow the reverse of the recommendations just noted for tax deferral activities.

Summary

This chapter provided the reader with a grounding in the essential tax issues pertaining to real estate investments. The general topics covered included real estate acquisitions, dispositions, and tax issues relating to personal residences. The tax code relating to these issues is exceedingly large, so it may be necessary to delve deeper into selected subject areas in order to gain a complete understanding of the applicable issues.

Glossary

A

Adjustable-rate mortgage. A mortgage with an interest rate that can change over time.

Adjusted basis. A change to the recorded initial cost of an asset after it has already been owned.

Appraisal. An expert estimate of the value of real estate.

B

Balloon loan. Any financing arrangement that includes a lump sum payment schedule at any point during its term.

Basis. The amount of capital investment in a property for tax purposes.

C

Capitalization rate. The rate of return that is expected to be generated on a real estate investment.

Coinsurance. An amount an insured must pay against a claim after the deductible is satisfied.

Common area maintenance charges. Charges paid by tenants on a proportional basis that are derived from their relative shares of the square footage in a building.

Condominium. A building containing a number of individually-owned apartments.

Consideration. Something of legal value that is given in exchange for a promise.

Cooperative. A form of shared housing in which each owner purchases a share of the entire building.

Credit report. A detailed breakdown of a person's credit history that is prepared by a credit bureau.

D

Deductible. The initial loss amount that must be absorbed by the insured party.

Depreciation. The planned, gradual reduction in the recorded value of an asset over its useful life by charging it to expense.

E

Earnest money deposit. A deposit made to a seller that represents a buyer's good faith to buy a property.

Escrow. A legal arrangement in which a third party temporarily holds a sum of money or property until a particular condition has been met.

F

Fixed-rate mortgage. A mortgage with an interest rate associated with it that remains constant over the entire term of the mortgage.

Foreclosure. The act of taking possession of a mortgaged property when the borrower fails to make scheduled mortgage payments.

G

Gross lease. When the lessor pays for nearly all of the operating expenses associated with a property.

Gross potential income. The maximum possible amount of income that a property can generate, assuming that it is fully leased out and all tenants are paying on time.

Gross profit. The selling price of a property minus its adjusted basis.

Gross rent multiplier. A metric used by real estate investors to evaluate potential investment properties.

J

Joint and several liability. When creditors can pursue a single general partner for the obligations of the entire business.

Joint tenancy. Co-ownership with a right of survivorship, which is most commonly associated with married couples.

L

Lease. An arrangement under which a lessor agrees to allow a lessee to use specified real property for a stated period of time in exchange for a series of payments.

Lease abstract. A summary of the most pertinent information within a lease.

M

Mailbox rule. The principle that an acceptance becomes effective and binds the offeror once it has been properly mailed.

Metropolitan statistical area. A geographical region with a relatively high population density at its core and close economic ties throughout the area.

Mid-month convention. When one-half of the normal depreciation rate is applied to the first and last months to be depreciated.

Modified gross lease. When lessees are responsible for some of the expenses incurred to run a property.

Mortgage. A loan used to buy real estate, for which that property then serves as collateral.

N

Negative amortization. An increase in the principal balance of a loan, which is caused by a failure to cover the interest due on the loan.

Net worth. Your assets minus your total liabilities.

Nonrecourse financing. When a lender cannot pursue an investor's personal assets for repayment of a loan.

O

Occupancy rate. The percentage of a property type that is currently being rented.

P

Points. The fees a borrower pays a mortgage lender to trim the interest rate on a loan.

Probate. The administration of a deceased person's will or the estate of a deceased person without a will.

R

Real estate. Land along with any permanent improvements attached to it, such as buildings and fences.

Real property business. Any operation that engages in the development, construction, acquisition, conversion, rental, operation, management, brokerage or leasing of real estate.

Recourse financing. When a lender can pursue an investor's personal assets for repayment of a loan.

Rent control. A government-imposed requirement that caps the amount of rent that can be charged on a property.

Rent roll. A list of the rent earned from each property unit.

Replacement cost. The cost that you would incur in order to build a comparable property in the same location, and which fulfills the same function.

Return on investment. The annual return generated from a property, divided into its purchase price.

S

Short sale. When a homeowner sells his or her property to a third party for less than the amount due on the associated mortgage, with all proceeds going to the lender.

T

Tenancy in common. Co-ownership where each party's ownership interest passes to that person's estate, rather than to the co-owner.

Timeshare. An arrangement under which several joint owners have the right to use a property as a vacation home under a time-sharing agreement.

Title insurance. A form of indemnity insurance that protects lenders and property purchasers from financial loss sustained from defects in the title to a property.

Triple net lease. When lessees are responsible for the payment of essentially all costs required to run a property.

Index

www.ingramcontent.com/pod-product-compliance
Lightning Source LLC
Chambersburg PA
CBHW051413200326
41520CB00023B/7222